M000023352

QUESTIONS OF FAITH

QUESTIONS OF FAITH
Contemporary Thinkers Respond

Edited by
Dolly K. Patterson

Trinity Press International
Philadelphia

First published 1990

Trinity Press International
3725 Chestnut Street
Philadelphia, PA 19104

All rights reserved. No part of this publication may be reproduced, stored in a retrieval system, or transmitted, in any form or by any means, electronic, mechanical, photocopying, recording or otherwise, without the prior written permission of the publisher, Trinity Press International.

©Trinity Press International 1990

Library of Congress Cataloging-in-Publication Data

Questions of faith: contemporary thinkers respond/edited by Dolly K. Patterson.
   p. cm.
   ISBN 0-334-02484-6
1. Faith. 2. Spirituality. 3. Theology, Doctrinal—Public opinion. I. Patterson, Dolly K.
BT771.2.Q55 1990
230—dc20   90-47636

Printed in the U.S.A.

Cover Photograph: Rancho de Taos Church by Martha Ley
Design & Production: Gail Hamilton

CONTENTS

ACKNOWLEDGMENTS

This book is based on the "Questions of Faith" video series developed and created by Jeff Weber and Peggy West for the Parish of Trinity Church (New York) and United Methodist Communications.

Executive Producers
Jeff Weber
Peggy West
Producers
Linda Hanick
Peggy West
Directors
Jack Hanick
Jay Voorhees
Interviewer
Jeff Weber
Associate Producers
Cherie Burns
Ed Gossard
Hilary Maddux
Assistant Producers
Leslie Alexander
Steve Downey
Camera
Lynn Allison
Bill Bliss
Marc Kroll
Ronny Perry
Joel Shapiro
David Werk
Audio
Lou Comentez
Kate Hudic
Lafayette Richardson
Post Production
On Track Video
Kopel Films
United Methodist Communications

EDITOR'S NOTE

Questions of Faith is like a box of Godiva chocolates, full of different kinds of appetizing satisfactions. Readers can choose from a variety of topics and a variety of speakers. The book can be read in one sitting or read randomly under different circumstances. Insights can be gained from simply reading one paragraph. This book is an ideal resource for the person who writes or who speaks publicly because of the breadth and depth of its material.

I have "digested" the material presented in this book in several ways—first, while using a tape recorder to record the conversations from the video series, which I then later played back and transcribed on my word processor. That was the easy part. Editing verbal conversations of such profound thinkers was at times intimidating, particularly the conversations of those who are also gifted writers. I tried to err on the conservative side and not take editorial liberties. I feel as if I have a personal relationship with many of these speakers because they have been so honest about their spiritual search and because I have spent so much time listening to their every word.

I want especially to thank Christopher Walters-Bugbee, editor of *Books and Religion* at Trinity Church in New York City, who first suggested this project to me. Chris is one of the most creative people I have ever met and has a great ability to guide professionally without controlling. Along with Chris, Jeffrey Weber and Linda Hanick, also of Trinity Church, and Harold Rast of Trinity Press, have impressed me with their personal integrity manifested in their professional lives.

Elizabeth Brady, my immediate supervisor at Church Divinity School of the Pacific, has kindly let me manipulate my work schedule to include projects like this one since I began working at CDSP in 1987. Virginia Hearn has been a mentor who has counseled me wisely on more than one occasion. Last, Caroline and Corwin Booth, my "surrogate family" in the Bay Area, loaned me their beach house for a week to finish this book—seven days that ended up being the best week of the summer for me.

Dolly Patterson
September 1990

INTRODUCTION

The idea to produce a video series like "Questions of Faith" came up during a dinner conversation I had with a colleague, Peggy West, in the summer of 1986. We were talking about how so many people we knew were reasking basic questions of belief and meaning and looking back over their shoulders at traditional concerns of faith. We both knew firsthand of people who, having lived through the turbulent sixties and selfseeking seventies, now found themselves in conversations in the most unlikely of places asking the most unlikely of questions: "What are you telling your kids about God?" "Do you pray?" "How do you know what's right?"

We also reflected how regrettable it was that those of us with such questions had few places to turn for help. For so many, traditional ways of addressing religious issues had lost meaning. Television had become a forum for religious discourse, but all too often it offered simplistic, pat answers, discouraging questioners from any real encounter with spiritual mystery. Peggy and I believed there were alternatives. We wanted to use media to introduce articulate, provocative thinkers grappling with the most difficult spiritual and religious themes.

The first series of televised interviews produced by United Methodist Communications asks questions like: "Who is God"? "What good is prayer?" "What's God got to do with evil?" "What's being good good for?" "Who needs organized religion?" "What matters anyway?" That series found outstanding reception in adult discussion groups within synagogues and churches of diverse faith groups. Based on its success, we followed with a second series coproduced with the Parish of Trinity Church (Episcopal), New York, and Linda Hanick joined us as producer. In this series we explored: "What's the use of the Bible?" "Who is Jesus?" "How do we right the wrong?" "Who's got the truth?" "What happens after death?" "What gives you faith?"

It has been a privilege to interview the extraordinary individuals who not only answered our audaciously huge questions with enthusiasm, but who were so honest about their personal lives.

In response to "What's your attitude toward death?" well-known author Madeleine L'Engle, speaking of her husband's death replied candidly, "When my husband was dying the church was wonderful. When he died, they had nothing to say. The old platitudes don't work." Nobel Peace Prize laureate, Desmond Tutu, reflected on the reality of death in his own life, revealing, "Yes, I think about death. You can't help thinking about death in South Africa when you get death threats frequently." And in response to "What's your image of God?" Korean theologian Hyung Kyung Chung shared her painful and oftentimes misunderstood struggle to rid herself of an image of God as "a white male disapproving grandfather who does not know me or my people."

Many of these guests welcomed the opportunity to rethink some of these very basic questions. T. George Harris, editor of *Psychology Today*, closed his interview (off camera) by saying "This is the toughest workout I've had in a long time." And when the Rt. Rev. John Spong, Episcopal Bishop of Newark, saw the completed video series, he commented that it was like "a personalized catechism."

This opportunity to extend the televised conversations into book form is exciting. Our hope has always been that these candid and courageous contemporary voices will encourage the rest of us to feel safe enough to examine our own moments of doubt and despair, knowing that those moments need not undermine our "conviction in things not seen."

Beyond the many insights offered in the following pages, these voices inspire us to dig for our own answers. They assure us of the value of the search.

Jeff Weber
September 1990

WHO IS GOD?

Will Campbell: I'm bothered by so many people who are so sure what God is up to, who God is, even what God looks like. There was never that kind of certainty in the beginning.

William Sloane Coffin: My image of God is of a very traditional, personalized deity. If we are going to experience God as a "personal power," we have to think of God in personal terms. It's quite right to call God "Father," although literally God is not father; or to address God as "Mother," although literally God is not mother.

For instance, the Spanish painter El Greco deliberately painted elongated fingers and noses, and distorted other human features to accentuate the mystery of human personality. Today we deliberately distort human relationships to avail upon the mystery of God by calling God "Mother" or "Father."

God represents love. When I pray to God, I feel the presence of a very personal power. You can't pray to the "unmoved mover" and feel very moved. I know what I'm doing when I pray to this type of God. Prayer likes this calls for an active imagination and is not literalism.

Madeleine L'Engle: Certainly I don't visualize God as looking like Moses losing his temper. When our children were little and we lived in northwest Connecticut, my husband and I experienced one tragedy after another for three years in a row. Four of our closest friends died. When something awful would happen, like one of these friends dying, we would pack the kids in the car and drive up to the top of Mohawk Mountain and wait for the stars to come out. That helped us put the tragedy in the context of a universe created by a loving God. At the time, my youngest concluded that all the galaxies, all the stars, and all of creation are "God's body." That's a wonderful image for me, because stars have always been numinous.

One of my first memories as a child is of visiting my grandmother at her beach cottage in North Florida during the days when you were tucked in bed with mosquito netting. One night after I had already gone to sleep, someone said, "Let's wake up the baby and show her the stars." They untucked the netting, carried me onto the beach, and there were the stars—the whole

*W*hen I pray to God I feel the presence of a very personal power. You can't pray to the "unmoved mover" and feel very moved.

William Sloane Coffin

universe was there. That was my first intuitive experience. I wasn't even two years old and was unable to articulate my experiences. But I remember understanding that I was glimpsing something far more wonderful and awesome than the ordinary daily life of a child, or indeed of any of us. So whenever I have attacks of faithlessness, which we all have occasionally, if I can see the stars, they will almost always bring me back to a sense of trust.

John Vannorsdall: From time to time my image of God is of an "old man in the sky." We all begin with primitive images. Part of Christian maturation is to move beyond traditional preconceptions, such as God being a male figure and the "old man in the sky," and to begin thinking of God in Jesus. It's even more important not to perceive God as being "up there" or "back there," but to see the God who was present in Christ when he lived on earth as still present now. Our imagination requires an image of God that Christians find in the teachings and events of Jesus.

Valerie Russell: It's important for us to get loose from our old patriarchal teachings of God and reconceptualize a variety of images of God. We need to see God as a part of nature, as a black or red or golden person, or as a woman, or as a cloud in the sky. We limit God's power in our lives by maintaining preconceived images.

I need to struggle to free my soul from those old images that are not helpful.

James Carroll: I depend on the Bible for my images. I think of the Bible as the language of my faith. The stories of Israel, the story of God liberating the people and insisting on freedom and revolution if it came to that; God as the faithful lover, as the one who suffers, as the ally of the poor—those are all important images. But even though those images sustain me in the faith, my religion does not depend on any one of them.

One of the things I cherish about the Bible is its ambivalent attitude toward images of God and how it always insists, even as it proposes images, that they should never be taken absolutely. Not even the image of

My religion does not depend on an image of God. One of the things I cherish about the Bible is its ambivalent attitude toward images.

James Carroll

3

Jesus should be interpreted as an absolute image of God. Biblical images are not definitive but suggestive.

Ignacio Castuera: I don't look at television when I want to pray, and I can't create images of God as a bearded patriarch or as Hera, the original earth mother and queen of the gods, during prayer either. I'm not able to create those types of images because what I'm desperately trying to do is to *listen*. I'm trying to find a connectedness. When I try to impose a theology of images, prayer becomes a projection of mine instead of an acceptance.

Harold Kushner: My Jewish tradition teaches me not to carry around images of God. One of the Ten Commmandments instructs us not to make an image of God, not to draw a picture of God, because you can define God too much. When you try to define God, automatically God comes in your mind as old not young, as male not female, as Caucasian not Hispanic or Asian. We Jews try to stay away from pictorial images of God and, rather, hold onto an image of God in action.

The important concept is not "*Where* is God, but *when* is God?" It's not about being in the right place, but the right thing happening—for example, helping a person across the street, giving charity, maintaining self-control. Those types of actions are examples of God in action. The act of kindness, the act of thoughtfulness, the act of self-discipline, all of these actions of human beings acting differently from the norm are a result of God's influence.

For me, those types of actions are key to what I think is the most obscure verse in all of scripture. In Exodus 33, when Moses asks to see God's face, the Lord tells Moses he can't see God's face, but he can see his back. Well, I don't believe that God really has a back. I think what God was telling Moses is that we too can't see God directly, face to face. But we can see God's after-effects. We can see the difference God makes in a person's life.

James Lawson: In our day and age, we need to increase our metaphors of God rather than limit them or try to put them in a single mold. As a pastor and preacher in a large congregation, I see a wide variety of people at different stages in their journeys. In some instances, using "God language" would be a handicap in communicating with them. For instance, our church has people with scientific backgrounds who need to be spoken to scientifically. Their thoughts about God tend to focus on the concept of energy rather than on a personal God. For communication purposes, sensitivity about "God language" is important.

Susan Schnur: I try to get away from a "Big God" focus. I'm more interested in interactive relationships and the sanctity of humans. Unfortunately, when you focus on sanctity of the deity, you sometimes de-sanctify other holy things. Part of my views are reactive as a Jew who lives in a Christian society. I don't want to feel so oppressed by the same God-emphasis that Christians have.

Mary Gordon: My images of God are so sappy and corny. It's as if they come from the jigsaw puzzles of Jesus and the children that I put together when I was five years old. My visual images just aren't very good.

I have more oral images of God, a harmonic image of God. I have a clear image of Jesus which probably comes from Cecil B. De Mille's movies. I believe that Jesus is divine, but my image of that divinity is of a human, not as God embodied. I have a tunnel image rather than a visual image of God; I think I know what God *sounds* like rather than what God looks like.

Will Campbell: Since I was a child, when someone brought up the name "God," I've thought about the story of Moses looking at the bush on fire. At first he probably thought it was a campfire, which wasn't particularly unusual at that time even though it was awfully hot. The bush wouldn't burn up though. Then the bush started talking, telling Moses to "Go here and tell these people this…and that…" which Moses accepted until all of a sudden he asked, "What if they ask who sent me?" which is basically asking the question, "Who is God?"

This voice, this God said, "Tell them that I AM sent you." Moses thought the voice was kidding, that the intelligent people he was supposed to talk to would never accept this story.

My images of God are so sappy and corny. It's as if they come from the jigsaw puzzles of Jesus and the children that I put together when I was five years old.

Mary Gordon

"I am who I am, sent you" this voice, this God image said.

So when someone asks me what I mean by "God," I mean God is God is God is God is God, period. Or, if I'm feeling particularly daring or reckless, I'll use a semicolon.

Peggy Way: God frequently comes to mind when I think about community because it seems that we have competing images of God in various communities. That's how God gets built into political wars and "holy wars." People justify wars by saying that God is involved. Persons have different images of God and are willing to battle for them.

I think all denominations have this mentality. It's not only the Southern Baptists who are being torn asunder. Theirs is an issue of "who is God" lying behind scriptural understanding. "Is it a God who dictates scripture?" "Is it a God who through human beings offers a variety of truthful perspectives?" There are battles about who God is that affect human community. Therefore it is important for me to have a variety of images about who God is, so I can invite others to understand my image and, at the same time, be able to hear their views.

Madeleine L'Engle: I remember a time of crisis when we were almost at war with Russia. Listening to the news, my husband and I couldn't hide from our children that we were anxious. That night we put our four-year-old son to bed, and he said his prayers—all the "God blesses"—aunts, uncles, cousins, animals, etc.—and all of a sudden he stopped in the middle and said, "And God, remember to be the Lord."

Afterward I thought, "I don't have to teach this child anything. He's got it all."

When the kids were little, I tried to answer questions they asked but not questions they didn't ask. Adults can make the mistake of answering too many other questions. If they'd ask me who God is, I probably would have said "God is love" and not gone on to answer the unasked questions.

WHAT GOOD IS PRAYER?

T. George Harris: I don't know exactly what prayer is. But for me it's the connection. There are many uncertainties. I can't tell you what God is, whether God has a beard or is a she, etc. But with prayer I do have a connection, which to me is a form of intense listening. When I go to church, I'm not too interested in what the preacher is saying, because what I'm doing there on my knees is trying to make that connection. Prayer is not television where I'm seeing or broadcasting. It's more like listening on a telephone. To the extent that I can move into an acceptance which allows me to hear, my whole body changes. I get a relaxation response (of which I can understand the physiology). But that's only part of the answer to what is going on when I pray. Prayer is profound acceptance.

A repetitive prayer I started using in World War II in combat when I'd go out on a reconnaissance, and was not sure whether I was going to come back, was "Not my will but thine." The capacity to give yourself to another reality than your own is essential for any religious experience. I have to start there.

William Sloane Coffin: Prayer, fundamentally, is an act of empathy, not an act of self-expression. Prayer is empathizing with God, trying to think God's thoughts with God, trying to see life from God's perspective. The word contemplation comes from "thinking with the temple." It's asking, "How would God look at this?"

Prayer is also an act of self-expression—that is, "God, feel the throbbing in my right knee." You have to be very specific. Some ministers think that dignity is attained at the expense of specificity. They would say, "God, here's my pain." But if you want to get somewhere, you're going to have to say, "God, feel the throbbing in my right knee."

Prayer is basically getting in touch with God.

Madeleine L'Engle: Everything we do, our whole interior monologue, is prayer. If I'm walking down the street thinking, "I'd really like to make some more money," that's prayer. It's not very good prayer, but it's prayer. We have a certain ability to direct how we pray.

I've memorized an alphabet of prayers that I like to use when I walk from my apartment to St. John the Divine Cathedral library. I can't pray

*E*verything we do, our entire interior monologue, is prayer. If I am walking down the street and thinking, "I'd really like to make more money," that's prayer. It's not very good prayer, but it's prayer.

Madeleine L'Engle

deeply on Broadway or I'll get hit by a bus. But at least if I walk along saying this alphabet of prayers, I'm stopping a lot of trivia from cluttering my mind.

Will Campbell: If God is this great mystery-being of awe, then this being is everywhere all the time. And if this God is, for example, omniscient, then every thought is a prayer, so there's not a time when I'm not praying. I think of God in these terms rather than in a compartmentalized way, such as saying, "Okay, it's God-time now."

John Vannorsdall: I rarely expect God to intervene in my life. When I was a kid, I spilled a box of nails in the garage. The next day was the school picnic, and I had promised that my mom would drive us. I prayed that night that God would see to it that there were no nails in the tires because the consequences would be disastrous for my image in that class. I haven't done that type of praying very often.

It's inappropriate to ask God to do things I ought to take care of or for which I ought to accept responsibility.

If we talk about a God of love, then God cares about how I feel. It's a part of my praise of God to share my needs, as well as the things that are going well, without expecting God to do anything—which is something God promises, not something God owes me.

James Carroll: For me, prayer mostly takes form of observing the rituals of the Catholic-Christian belief. It doesn't often take the form of talking to God. I kneel down regularly to pray with my children. We say our "God bless mommy, God bless daddy" prayers. I am scrupulous in teaching them, because I want my kids to be at home in handing over to the care of God the things that matter.

I pray ordinarily by willfully observing the ritual moments in life. They comprise, in fact, the sacramental moments. The Eucharist is central. My attachment to the Mass, my hunger for it as a basic prayer, is what keeps me Catholic. But I treasure all the sacraments.

Last year my wife and I had a daughter who died shortly after she was born. The baby's name was Jenny. After a traumatic delivery, the doctors put her on a machine to help her breathe. She needed to catch the habit of breathing or she would die. At that point I had an absolutely instinctive wish to baptize her—that is to say, to pray for her.

I asked for a cup of water (a nurse thought I was going to faint). There's nothing in my belief that made it essential that this baby be baptized, as if this baby's fate was going to be changed. But it seemed crucial to baptize her, because it was my way of representing everyone who loved her, of putting her in the presence of all those others, including especially God. Baptizing Jenny was making explicit what was already true, that we all loved her so much. That God did.

Saying that simple prayer, signing the cross, pouring water, was a release for her and for me. It was a basic act of handing over to the care of God what matters most—an act, as I say, of prayer.

Valerie Russell: Prayer is a time when you call on the Spirit, for healing. It's also a time when you meditate to get in touch with the seeds of power within you, which is not asking God to do something for you but to empower you to do something for yourself. For me, after I've gotten that sense of the power within me and the discernment of what I should do, prayer is going out and doing what you need to do. Prayer is standing in a picket line or sitting down and trying to talk with a prisoner who's just tried to commit suicide.

Prayer is any interaction where you need the Spirit and try to lift up the problem or issue that needs healing.

Harold Kushner: Prayer is not going to God with your shopping list. Save that for Santa Claus. I'll violate my own rule against defining it, if you promise not to take my definition too seriously. Prayer for me is talking in the presence of God, not so much talking to God or with God, but talking in God's presence. Because when you understand that you're talking in God's presence, you become different. Even when you leave God's presence, you're different because of that experience.

Eskimos have twenty-five words for snow because snow is an important part of their lives. If prayer were an important part of our lives, we'd have a lot more words for it. To use the word "prayer" to mean a weekly

*P*rayer is a time when you meditate to get in touch with the seeds of power within you, which is not asking God to do something for you but to empower you to do something for yourself.

Valerie Russell

congregational service or personal reflection or the desperate gasp of asking for help in a hospital room, that's stretching the same word too far. Those are all different phenomena.

For me congregational prayer, joining with others to create the moment when God is present, is one very specific experience. Acknowledging my own limitations and admitting that the most important things in my life—my health, the well-being of my family, getting people to love me, world peace—these things are not in my power to bring about. I have to turn to some other power beyond myself. That's a very different kind of religious experience.

The desperate reaching out—"Don't let me feel that I am alone at a time like this"—is still another type of prayer.

James Lawson: Prayer is deeds of concern for the neighbor; actions on behalf of justice are prayer. Prayer is trying to let your life be open to the channels of God's love and purpose. That kind of opening of life, of keeping doors, windows, attitudes, your mind, and your heart open to God, is prayer.

Susan Schnur: In the Jewish tradition prayer is always done in community and is programmatic. In a Friday night service when we pray, what we are getting is a sense of being instead of doing, a sense of having a model through repetition which can be transcending. Sabbath is the time to be instead of do—at-oneness, which we call atonement. It's somehow entering into a different relationship with the world so that you're not confrontational, not exploiting. Prayer gives you a context to do that.

Daniel Matthews: Prayer is not so much getting what you want, like "God please give me a parking place." That's a corruption. It happens, and we do pray like that. But prayer centers in loving God, turning one's whole countenance over to the presence of God in your life.

When you fall in love, you don't think first of all, "I want to ask that person for something." You want to be with that person, you just want to

That kind of opening of life, of keeping doors, windows, attitudes, your mind, and your heart open to God, is prayer.

James Lawson

spend time with that person. Prayer is spending time with God. That's the essence of prayer.

Ignacio Castuera: From a Christian perspective, prayer for others is the most important. Prayer for ourselves is important but not as important as praying for others. Look at our model—the Lord's Prayer—or even at the shortest prayer in the Bible, "What do you want me to do?"—those are prayers on behalf of others rather than, "Just do this for me." Some people believe in a kind of magical formula for prayer that is similar to "tit for tat": If I just say the right things or do the right things, God will act on my behalf. Religious people walk a thin line between prayer and that type of thinking. I prefer to stay away from the magical and move more in the direction of looking for possible answers or extra help at a time of perplexing circumstances.

Valerie Russell: I'm most likely to pray for strength and power within myself to do frightening things I don't want to do. People who are seriously trying to live on the cutting edge—trying to be a bridge between communities of black/white, suburban/urban, rich/poor—have a lonely time of it. Sometimes you feel isolated by both sides. Bridges don't stand in the middle; they have to straddle both sides. It's a lonely place. There are times when I want to sit in Hawaii and look at the surf, or find a job in a corporation and make a lot of money and not worry about social issues. I usually pray not to give in to the hopelessness that I feel around me and to find the kind of resilience that enables me to do hard tasks.

Madeleine L'Engle: When I ask for prayers, I don't know what I expect. When Hugh, my husband, had cancer, I called people for prayer. All I know that happened was that the prayers certainly sustained me and gave me strength to get through a long period of time. I needed strength beyond my own. When Hugh died, one of our godchildren said, "But the prayers didn't work."

"Yes, they did. They don't always work in the way we hope and plan and wish," I said.

I'm less and less specific in my intercessory prayers. I have a couple of friends with cancer and all I say is, "God, here is Connie." I'm less and less specific in my demands.

Toward the end of Hugh's illness someone asked, "How shall we pray?"

"Pray for what is best for Hugh," I said.

Mary Gordon: My father used to make fun of my mother and say, "My wife prayed for a black Oldsmobile and she got one." There seems to be a kind of elitism about prayer which I really don't like. Most of the world prays for some kind of reward. It makes me nervous to compare and think, "My prayer is a good kind of prayer, because my prayer is adoration, not petition, and yours is, 'Can I please get rid of this ingrown toenail.'"

I'm just nervous about these kinds of questions in general.

Ignacio Castuera: When people pray that the consequences of certain sins not happen, that's not prayer. That's incantation—you do the right motions or say the right words, and God is going to change something as if God is a reacting kind of being.

But I'd have a hard time with a God whose mind can be changed, who can stop the rules of nature just on my behalf. I would feel proud and haughty to think that God would stop the whole world on my behalf, that God would stop the normal growth of cancer cells in my mother's body just for my sake. I'd rather think of God as someone who's going to provide me with strength and power to endure those situations rather than to reverse those situations.

William Sloane Coffin: One shouldn't expect to know specific answers to specific questions often. If you and I were conversing, I wouldn't expect you to give me all the answers to my problems. I'd like you to give me a ready ear. I'd like to feel that you heard me. That's what one hopes from God and can expect. That's what Jesus prayed when he said, "Let this cup pass from me." He didn't think God was necessarily going to let that happen, but he was expressing his desire. It was a perfect prayer: "Let this cup pass from me; nevertheless, not my will but thine be done." "Oh God, get me out of this horrible mess; nevertheless, if I have to stay in it, help me to do something creative with it."

We've confused God with Santa Claus. We've been taught that if we ask urgently enough and if we've been a good boy or girl, we'll get it. That's just not the way the world works.

Harold Kushner

One shouldn't pray to God with specific problems for specific answers as if God were some Greek oracle or medium or channel. Rather one goes to God to find strength beyond oneself, to find "a peace that passeth all understanding." There's a lot more to this world than oneself. We have to find wisdom from God rather than smart answers to tough questions.

Peggy Way: I always expect God to change something—that's a human response. Why have a God if you can't talk God into changing something? I may want God to change my husband or my path or the state of today's world.

Hopefully, one of the positive things we learn in prayer is that one cannot manipulate God any more than one can manipulate human beings.

Harold Kushner: We've been badly taught about prayer. We've confused God with Santa Claus. We've been taught that if we've been a good boy or girl and if we ask urgently enough, we'll get it. That's just not the way the world works.

My favorite prayer in the Bible is the one Jacob offers just before wrestling with the angel in the Book of Genesis. He's at the same river bank where, as a teenager, he had prayed a very immature prayer: "Keep me safe, make me rich, and I will thank you and worship you like crazy." Now, twenty years later, he comes back much more mature. There's no bargaining; there's no Santa Claus list.

His prayer is: "I have to do something hard; I know it's right and I'm not sure I can do it. If you help me, maybe I can do it. If you leave me on my own, I know I'll fall on my face the way I have every other time I've tried to do this." For me, that's prayer. It doesn't change the world. Jacob is about to meet his brother Esau who has said, "The next time I meet you, I'm going to kill you." Jacob doesn't ask God to turn Esau into a pussycat. He doesn't ask God to strike Esau with amnesia so he'll forget his anger.

Rather, Jacob says to God: "I've spent my whole life running from confrontation. I'm tired of running. Help me face up to this and get through this crisis."

That's prayer. *Don't change the world. Don't take away the problems. Don't make my road smooth. But give me the grace to walk it, no matter how rocky it is.*

WHAT'S GOD GOT TO DO WITH EVIL?

God doesn't want a young wife/mother to be struck down with multiple sclerosis. God doesn't want a family to be killed by a drunk driver in a traffic accident. I have to believe that these things do not represent the will of God.

Harold Kushner

Harold Kushner: The question of why God permits suffering is the fundamental religious question. It's the only question people care about at a gut level. Everything else is intellectual games.

God doesn't want a young wife/mother to be struck down with multiple sclerosis. God doesn't want a family to be killed by a drunk driver in a traffic accident. I have to believe that these things do not represent the will of God.

So why do these things happen? They happen sometimes because laws of nature don't make exceptions for nice people. We are as subject to illness and accident as anybody else. They happen sometimes because God will not take away our humanity by taking away our right to decide how we want to live and what we want to do. Human beings cause some disasters, laws of nature cause others. But they're not the will of God.

If I have to choose between an all-powerful God who is not fair and kind, who lets innocent people suffer, who *wants* them to suffer, or else a good and kind God who is not all-powerful—as a religious person I would rather affirm God's goodness at the expense of God's power and not insist on an omnipotent God.

We don't add to God's glory by insisting that disasters are "God's will." Who would worship a God who *wants* little children to drown or who wants people to die in agony? Such happenings cannot possibly be the will of God—or not any God I would be concerned with worshiping.

Mary Gordon: The question of evil and a loving or unloving God has arisen personally for me today. I came to this interview after the funeral of a thirty-five-year-old woman, the mother of my children's friend. She died of breast cancer, leaving her two little girls and husband behind. Why is a loving God allowing that to happen? Did God "need" that woman? Did God "need" that suffering?

I prefer to think of tragic events as happening randomly, rather than perceiving God as saying, "Oh, well, they might really be helped by death. And terminal cancer would do her a world of good." That type of thinking about God is really dreadful.

I have absolutely no good answer to the problem of evil in this world. It is the central problem for religious people.

William Sloane Coffin: A lot of terrible events have happened that we can't in any way blame God for. My son Alex died because he hadn't had the windshield wiper fixed on his car, the rain was coming down hard, there were no lamps on the road by the Boston Harbor, and he took the wrong road and went into the harbor. But that was clearly human error.

When the parents of the Marines who were killed in Lebanon appeared on television, many of them said, "Well, this must have been the will of God for my son to die." As if God "willed" the United States Marine Corps to go to Lebanon in the first place. I'm astonished that people can lose their son in war and say, "It's the will of God."

The question of why there's evil in this world is the central problem for religious people.

Mary Gordon

17

All war is rooted in human pride and human error. I picture Jesus standing between the lines of battle with each bullet going through his body.

For cancer to strike someone early in life is what I mean by the suffering of the innocent. I don't think there's any good answer for why that type of suffering exists.

Christians make a big mistake when they try to pretty up a terrible tragedy by saying "Well, this is the will of God." We don't know why tragedy happens sometimes, and we'd better say we don't know when we don't.

Madeleine L'Engle: This question is central to understanding the nature of creation and the creator. I don't have any answers. I just know that sometimes incredibly wonderful things happen, and sometimes incredibly terrible things happen, and we don't know why.

Sometimes during those terrible times I'm inclined to cry out, "My God! My God! Why have you forsaken me?" To feel that way is all right.

Harold Kushner: Spinoza said, "God is not coextensive with nature." God is moral. God knows the difference between good people and bad ones. Nature doesn't. Nature is blind. So nature hurts people with illness, with AIDS, with viruses, with infections, with falling rocks, with earthquakes. But God recognizes a good person in pain and tries to comfort and give solace to that hurting person.

Susan Schnur: Where one should be looking for answers regarding evil is at humans. How did people let something like a genocide happen? Putting the responsibility on humans is more useful and realistic and, frankly, gives me more faith. I'm certainly aware that historically God has been used as often negatively as positively. As a Jew with any sense of history, and especially in light of two thousand years of church history, I'm as frightened by someone who is "God-fearing" as I am comforted.

James Carroll: The great religious question of our time, of course, is how to believe in God after Auschwitz. Despite the horrible irony of it, I think

Christians make a big mistake when they try to "pretty up" a terrible tragedy by saying, "Well, this is the will of God." We don't know why tragedies happen sometimes, and we better say we don't know when we don't.

William Sloane Coffin

that Auschwitz prepares us at last to truly believe in God. Now we can no longer maintain the childish notion that God is the one who does good things for us, that God is supposed to act as a kind of supershield delivering us from evil. On the contrary, the God of the Bible is the God who allows the most unimaginable things to happen, up to and including the crucifixion of Jesus. Biblical people often experience God as the enemy. At the end, if only for a moment, Jesus seemed to feel that way. After Auschwitz, perhaps we do too. But this is the very wall through which biblical faith pushes. God is not the enemy who causes evil. God is the mysterious friend who stands with us in its midst.

Madeleine L'Engle: How can we believe in a loving God in a world where the innocent suffer and the wicked flourish? That question makes a lot of people atheists.

Evil was put into real context for me when my actor-husband played the father in the play, *The Diary of Anne Frank.* Our children were seven, ten, and twelve when we went to see it after having read the book. Watching the story on stage was an incredible point of rethinking for us. The family was hiding in the attic when Hitler was collecting the Jews to send to prison camps. In the climax, it was Hanukkah, and Anne had made gifts for everyone because, of course, they had not been able to buy any presents. They're happy and merry and allowed to talk because no one is downstairs. All of a sudden there's a terrible crash on the first floor. When the father gets up and goes down to investigate, they know he may never come back. The mother drops on her knees in a great plea, crying out the 121st Psalm: "The Lord shall preserve thy going out and thy coming in from this time forth...." But the Lord didn't do that. God didn't preserve that family. They were taken by the Nazis, put in a concentration camp, and all of them died there except the father.

After the play my kids were outraged and asked, "Why did Anne Frank have to die?"

"Because the Nazis caught the family and put them in concentration camps, " I said.

"But it wasn't right!" they protested.

"No. It was terribly wrong, but it happened."

"But it wasn't fair!"

We had never pretended to our kids that it was a fair world, but this was a kind of unfairness beyond anything they'd ever dreamed of.

One of them finally said, "Well, if God lets things like that happen, then I don't want God."

I understand that reaction.

I've heard it said that the Holocaust will make us either atheists or committed believers. That is because God has given us free will, and when we abuse our freedom, we can't go thumping in on God. Anne Frank suffered from the Nazis' abusive free will, and that probably goes back a hundred years previously to other events where people abused free will.

Watching that play maybe a dozen times was very important in my thinking about how much we can demand of God without being puppets. If we've been given free will, we have to accept the consequences that follow our actions.

John Vannorsdall: The God who is always messing around in my life, pulling the strings, and causing things to happen or not happen—that God I don't want. I become angry at a God who would treat me in that way, or demean my responsibility as a person who can be accountable. Part of my maturation in faith has been learning to appreciate the distance-keeping of God at times, which I don't interpret as negative or as indifference on God's part, but rather as an act of love.

If I live on a flood plain and it's raining and flooding my house, it's my fault, not God's, because I chose to live on that flood plain. If I am part of the polluting of the food we eat and the water we drink, and I become ill from it, it's my fault, not God's.

I remember one day watching my daughter trying to change a tire. I knew she was turning the nut the wrong way. I watched her from a distance and decided to walk past her and go out to the barn, hoping she would ask me for help. But instead she said nothing when she saw me

The God who is always messing around in my life, pulling the strings, and causing things to happen or not happen—that God I don't want.

John Vannorsdall

approach her. I waited a while in the barn and couldn't stand it any longer.

Finally I said, "You're turning the nut the wrong way."

She simply exploded: "I know why you walked to the barn. You couldn't help yourself. You had to interfere. I am *learning* how to change this tire."

I understood that. She had a right to be angry. I had denied her integrity and accountability by not giving her the opportunity to learn by herself.

When we postulate a God who is always interfering, it is like a father who butts in when his daughter is learning to change a tire. God doesn't desert us in our learning-times. I think my daughter would have been happy to know that if things really fell apart, I would comfort her. But it was important for her maturation to have control and change that tire by herself.

That kind of human autonomy, of learning how to do something for oneself but knowing that comfort is available from God, is different from the concept a lot of people have about who God is. But it's the only God to whom I can relate.

Is God in control? I hope not. The world is a mess. I believe that God is in control ultimately.

Ignacio Castuera

James Carroll: I'd have to turn my experience of human life inside out to believe God was in charge of this world. Certainly God is not in charge in the sense of controlling what happens, either in our daily lives or across the sweep of history.

By definition, history is at the mercy of human choices and acts of nature which no one controls. For instance, who's "in charge" when nature throws up a deadly virus that is unprecedented? Or when a mad ruler launches a genocidal war? Or, for that matter, when a lover unexpectedly walks out of your life?

Notes of chaos and absurdity have to coexist in human life with the belief that God loves us; our very freedom from control is, in fact, a sign of that love.

Ignacio Castuera: Is God in control? I hope not. The world is a mess. I believe that God is in control *ultimately.* But God is one power among other powers. I've not believed that God was omnipotent since I was a child and my mother told me in Spanish that "God cannot remove a spanking." That's true. God doesn't remove a spanking. The brute fact of the past is far more powerful than God.

William Sloane Coffin: We have to take human freedom very seriously, which means if we're free to do good, we're also free to do evil. Our wills are basically flawed. Intelligence is not going to turn selfishness around, although it may make it a little more enlightened. But intelligence cannot make us selfless. Our wills are too self-centered to change much.

Because it's very hard to be selfless, we need the help of religion. People who try to be selfless on their own, without God's help, demonstrate how little they live out their convictions. Evil is basically sinfulness, and is serious, and is an obvious fact of life.

The doctrine of original sin is one of the most optimistic doctrines the church has ever promulgated in the sense that it tells us, "Don't feel desperate. You're not supposed to be a Girl Scout."

Will Campbell: God created the world and gave it to us. We're pretty much in charge of it in this era.

Some people think I am in a state of despair, but I'm not. Because even if we exercise our freedom to the point of blowing up the universe, which we are free to do and are capable of doing, that is not going to be the last word.

Being convinced of that is enough to keep me going.

WHAT'S BEING GOOD GOOD FOR?

Mary Gordon: A good person is someone who is genuinely loving and selfless and open, qualities that I find rare and nearly impossible to achieve for more than five minutes in my own life. But I have met people like that. There's a kind or porosity to them. When I am in their presence I feel understood, taken in, apprehended in some very full way.

> *Goodness is a way of living directly and lovingly in an ambiguous world.*
>
> *James Carroll*

Valerie Russell: Good persons are open to hearing other people. They don't always operate out of their own lives and from their own agenda. They can respond and interact with me and with other people.

It's interesting that in our society, where everything is so instant, interpersonal relationships of depth suffer so much. We run from friendship to friendship and don't tell our stories to one another very easily.

Anelle Morton, a feminist theologian, said, "We can hear one another into being." We can tell our stories to one another and learn from each other's experience.

T. George Harris: The Aquinian concept of original sin is self-concern and self-centeredness. Good people are able to transcend themselves and move beyond being self-centered to giving themselves totally to a spontaneous moment.

James Carroll: I think that goodness is a way of living directly and lovingly in an ambiguous world. For a writer, that means being faithful to writing. For a politician, that means being politically astute. But the world is ambiguous for everyone, and knowing that, we should be very reluctant to pass absolute judgment on the "goodness" of others. The tradition is wise to leave that business to God.

Peggy Way: A good person is not fully described by contemporary psychology because the focus there is mainly on being "liberated." Of course, inner freedom can be healthy and constructive. But I'd take the definition further and say that a good person is one who is liberated in order to live justly and to serve the community.

Ignacio Castuera: When I think about good people, I think about people who are involved in justice work because they are trying to convey the love of God. Whenever that love of God is thwarted or stopped by any force or any person, then these good people stand up and struggle for that love to continue. Mother Teresa is one of those persons. Martin Luther King was another. Bishop Tutu is still another.

Will Campbell: I don't know much about good people. When that subject came up, Jesus said, "Hey, why are you calling me good? There's none good but God." We all say things like "Pete O'Cross is a good neighbor." Well, we say he's a good neighbor because he lets me borrow his chain saw. And when my tractor breaks down, he brings his over and helps me plow my fields.

For most of us, goodness is a relative term: there's something in it for me. But when Jesus said, "There is none good," including himself, then I would be hard pressed to claim I'm a good guy.

Harold Kushner: Religion offers us the definition of what a good person looks like. A colleague of mine says, "What religion gives us is not theology but biography." Religion does not give us abstract rules but living examples of persons struggling with frustrations, with anger, with temptation to take things that don't belong to them. The heroes of the Bible are not plaster saints. They have problems with their marriages, with their children, and with other ethical situations. Abraham lied. Jacob lied. David did shameful things. Yet somehow they were able to surmount those offenses and give us examples of how we can be good even though we're not perfect.

Religion assures us that what we do matters to God, that God notices even if nobody else does. Nobody knows that I was tempted to shoplift and didn't. Nobody knows when I was tempted to say something cruel and hurtful but held back. But God knows. No good deed ever goes wasted.

Mary Gordon: Sometimes religion can get in the way of living a moral life. People think that their morality is taken care of because, for an hour a

Sometimes religion can get in the way of living a moral life because it makes people think their morality is taken care of.

Mary Gordon

week, they think about the good.

Religion also gets in the way of goodness when people have an "us versus them" mentality. A lot of religious people feel, "We are saved, you are not; we can talk only to ourselves, we can't talk to you." They have a sense that they are superior because of their religious life.

But religion doesn't *have* to get in the way. These things are tremendously random.

Susan Schnur: Religion clearly has a lot to do with being a good person, but it depends on how you package it. You can use your religion to become more dogmatic and less open to other people's perception. It's not intrinsic that religion will bring about goodness, but it does have that potential. You can look at the injunction of your faith in ways that can help guide you in good behavior.

Valerie Russell: Even though we take a chance about what happens after this life, I try to be a good person because God calls us to use all of our humanity. People who try to live open to the Spirit and who seek goodness live far richer lives than those who live hunkered-down, fearful lives, isolated in homogeneous situations, and who can't be open to newness and change. My life is rich because I'm trying to be open.

The answer is yes and no to the question, "Does being good reap rewards?" because there is a reward in the quality of one's life—but not an outward, tangible reward.

Harold Kushner: What's the payoff for trying to be a good person? The Talmud teaches us that the only reward for a good deed is that it makes the next good deed easier. God doesn't draw a magic circle around you to protect you and make sure disaster doesn't happen to you, but it does happen to the next guy. I don't think that any of the rewards for living a "good" life come our way with such guarantees.

You won't necessarily live a happier, longer life as a result of being good. There's an old joke about a man who asks his rabbi, "If I stop drinking and gambling and running around, will I live longer?"

"No, but it will feel longer," the rabbi replies.

William Sloane Coffin: The notion that goodness will be rewarded is without doubt the most cherished middle-class notion there is. Nonetheless, to live with the idea that you will be rewarded is to invite all kinds of disappointment. My philosophy is: "No good deed goes unpunished," and I think that's rather biblical.

Jesus, for his pains, was rejected by all his disciples bar none, and was crucified and forgotten. Paradoxically, he did it all for "the joy that was set before him." What does "joy" mean? Who wants to be crucified? Being hung on a cross was joyful?

I think that "joy" there refers to fulfillment, which is not necessarily happiness. Happiness comes indirectly as a byproduct of a certain quality life. Joy is a result of living a life of integrity.

We would never have crucified Christ had we not crucified the best within us. People don't like to be reminded of what they have crucified within themselves.

One of the first things that drew me to Christianity was this deep, realistic understanding that life is basically very tragic. It's not that human beings hate evil so much as it is that we hate the good in the world because it's so demanding of us, and therefore we repress it.

Will Campbell: I hope to love my neighbor as myself, though I'm quite sure I don't do that most of the time. I hope I will not kill someone, but I know I do constantly as a citizen of a very nationalistic and militaristic nation. I know that I helped kill Moammar Khadafy's fourteen-month-old child.

Now what do I do when I realize that I'm a murderer and hater, that I don't love my neighbor as myself, that I violate all the commandments?

Well, I understand grace and its significance in my life. Does this mean that I am free to do anything I want to do because of grace—that I can keep on not caring? No, understanding grace does not send me into a state

The notion that goodness will be rewarded is without doubt the most cherished middle-class notion there is.

William Sloane Coffin

of inactivity and indifference. It sends me into the streets caring for humanity in response to grace.

Madeleine L'Engle: As far as I'm concerned, there's only one absolute: God is love. As a flawed human being, I don't know all that much about love. I know I loved one man for forty years. I love my children and grandchildren. But there's a lot about love I don't know. I'm still learning.

William Sloane Coffin: Yes, the one absolute is love. The integrity of love is much more important than the purity of dogma. Dogma is a signpost, not a hitching post. It's always pointing beyond itself to God. My problem with fundamentalists is that they put the purity of dogma ahead of the integrity of love and end up quite loveless in many instances.

Also, you can build community out of seekers of truth, but you can't build community out of possessors of truth because they're also possessed of a certain enmity toward those who don't possess the truth.

We worship a God of such divine incomprensibility that to say we speak for God takes more gall than we should allow ourselves. We should only say, "In my best thought and deepest feeling, this is the way it ought to be."

Love is a plumb line that measures all these things. If we believe in that type of God, our faith doesn't necessarily clear up uncertainty, but it makes it possible to live with it. We can stand both intellectual uncertainty and moral ambiguity. We don't have to hang on to absolute truths with a white-knuckle grip. We can be available for deeper meanings that may come our way.

WHO NEEDS ORGANIZED RELIGION?

James Carroll: The organized church, despite all its flaws and blind spots, is what enables one generation to learn the story and pass it down to the next. That's all we mean by the church. If there was no church we wouldn't have the story.

The Bible which tells the story exists in a community. That community is the church.

Madeleine L'Engle: When I speak at denominational universities, I'm often asked what I think of the organized church. My answer is, "I think it stinks, but it's all we've got." You can't do it in isolation. There's got to be community. The problem is that churches and temples no longer are the communities they were intended to be. We no longer recognize Christians by how they love, but rather by how they condemn. Being judgmental is a bad way to be recognized.

I have a friend who became an alcoholic as a teenager. She then spent ten years as a young adult participating in Alcoholics Anonoymous. She was thirty years old and planned on driving from New York to California alone. I felt greatly concerned about her doing this. It was an awfully long trip to take alone.

She said, "Don't worry. If I'm lonely, I'll just call AA." I thought, "If I'm driving across the country and I call the local church saying 'I'm lonely,' how would they respond?" (Probably a telephone-answering machine would pick up the call.) It's likely that I'm not going to get as much compassion as if I had called AA—which is a terrible indictment of the church.

I'm very involved with the institutional church. But I think we are not fulfilling our obligation to be communities within communities within communities.

Harold Kushner: What religion offers me is not fellowship with God, but fellowship with other human beings who are looking for the same things I am. Loneliness is today's greatest spiritual problem. People who have no intention of shopping go to shopping centers because they need to be where other people are. People come home and turn on the television set,

*W*hat religion offers is not fellowship with God, but fellowship with other humans who are looking for the same things I am.

Harold Kushner

not to watch the program, but to hear another human voice because they're lonely.

Religion should offer us that sense of community, that sense of "Here are people who share something important with you." You don't come to church or temple to find God—you can find God on a mountaintop or in your bedroom. You come to church or temple to find a congregation, to find others who need the same things from life that you need. By coming together, you create the moment together where God is present. This is the one indispensable thing that organized religion offers us, which our vague individual sense of spirituality cannot.

William Sloane Coffin: If Christ is God's love in person on earth, churches ought to be God's love in an organization on earth. If love is what it's all about, where are we going to celebrate this love unless in community with loving people? Essentially what a church or temple ought to be is a community of loving people who believe that our lives consist of an abundance of love—not of an abundance of possessions.

It would be nice to say to people, "If you want to know something about Judaism, here's a temple you can visit." "If you want to know something about Christianity, here's a church for you to attend." Essentially that is the way it ought to be. But there's a big difference between what we are existentially and what we are essentially.

Peggy Way: From my point of view, one of the central theological issues is "How do we make that big leap from local to global?" At its best, the local church offers a sense of community. So the idea of community doesn't mean that everyone in the church loves each other. Even in the local church there are "obnoxious" people who don't have the "right" point of view. More realistically, the local church is a place where people can learn how to stand one another. Notice I didn't say love each other. I said stand each other. In our culture, this may be one of the most important things the church offers: models, images, experiences of how we tolerate others who differ from us.

If the ecumenical movement, local churches, and various denomina-

If Christ is God's love in person on earth, churches ought to be God's love in an organization on earth.

William Sloane Coffin

tions took this seriously, the church could become the only institution that intentionally helped people learn to live with one another despite their differences. That's a central theological issue for the twenty-first century.

James Lawson: Religion is the effort to organize goodness and compassion and love. It's why Moses organized his people to campaign against slavery. It's why Jesus clearly called all sorts of people to come together and experience a new humanity to try to turn the world upside down.

Where in today's world do you find an institution that proclaims that the nuclear race must end and that arms be subverted to the priority of the people's needs, as the Catholic and Methodist bishops did? Chase Manhattan Bank doesn't say that. Corporations don't say that.

Where do we hear an institution proclaim that "everyone is loved by God and therefore is somebody of great worth"? That's the message you hear in our churches and synagogues week after week, and in religious writings, not in the governments of the world or in the White House.

Organized religion is God's deliberate intention for people to come together and recognize that they have a strength to oppose evil, and in their unity, to transform the earth. They have this strength together, not apart.

Yes, I clearly recognize that if we did not have churches and synagogues, we'd have to invent them, so indeed some people could organize their lives around the values that make life whole.

Valerie Russell: The church doesn't raise its outcry in rage and ask society to confront the basic moral value-questions that nobody else is facing. Only an organized people who've struggled with a vision can do this.

Will Campbell: I'm suspicious of anything that is organized or institutionalized because sooner or later every institution comes to exist for its own sake, for its own growth, for its own well-being, for those who are profiting by it. In other words, all institutions are inherently evil by the very definition of the word.

Where do we hear an institution proclaim that "everyone is loved by God and therefore is somebody of great worth"? That's the message you hear in our churches and synagogues week after week, and in religious writings, not in the governments of the world or in the White House.

James Lawson

T. George Harris: You can often see the church as the public health nurse. It gives you an inoculation of a de-nurtured "religiosity," one that kills the virus so you won't catch the real thing. You can see the church protecting us against a real infection of religion. A lot of folks send their kids to Sunday school these days to be sure they won't get mixed up with the Moonies or with some other eccentric group; you have to "protect" them against that kind of religion. The church has always had this role, but it seems to be doing it more now than in the past.

Mary Gordon: Paradoxically one benefit of organized religion is that it is less exclusive than unorganized religious groups simply because it has buildings and a set time to show up and a means of facilitating strangers. I would not like to see all religious organizations disappear, because too much would then be left to chance. I'm not interested in the organization of organized religion per se, but I think its rituals are essentially a public happening that takes place in community.

There is a great temptation to try to have a spiritual life without being in community. It's much easier because you don't have to deal with someone who believes the same things you do even though you don't like her or him personally. It's just you and God and Kierkegaard. The company is very elite. That's dangerous. Organized religion prevents this type of nullified relationship, which is important.

James Carroll: Most everyone I know and certainly most of the people I like being around have rejected the church. I haven't, perhaps because my expectations of the church are different from theirs. I don't expect the church to be exempt from our flawed, struggling, limited human experience.

Many people, including me at times, are angry at the church and at religious leaders for various hypocrisies. But often we're angry because we expect them to be immune, much like a child expects a parent to be immune, from what it means to be a human being. The church is not immune. It brings such anger on itself, of course, because for generations the church has claimed for itself exactly this kind of special status.

One of the terrible mistakes of the Catholic tradition is the idea of the infallibility of the pope, which is a meaningless notion. Theologians have to stand on their heads to explain it in some way that has any meaning. The doctrine of infallibility amounts to announcing the church's exemption from the limitations of human life. When people discover that the church is not exempt at all, they become furious at it and leave.

John Vannorsdall: I see all the difficulties of the organized church. But where else do you hear in a systematic, ongoing, rhythmic way the witness about what God is doing in human history? Where else does a group of people pause to reflect on their lives in the presence of that witness concerning God? Call it confession. Call it praise. But where else do we have the incarnation of values via hymns, prayers, rituals, stained glass windows, and buildings?

People who say they can make it spiritually without community deny that religion is essentially always community. People who say they can do without the institutionalized church fool themselves about the physical nature of the embodiment that is their own lives.

HOW DO YOU DEAL WITH RELIGIOUS DIFFERENCES?

Ignacio Castuera: The question of whether all religions are the same is difficult for Christians to address because Christians, especially in the nineteenth century, claimed we were number one and there was no other truth. Certainly one can point to verses in the Bible to justify that point of view, such as "outside of Christ there is no salvation," etc.

In the world in which we now live, we must try to live in dialogue with people of other religions. We must try to be more humble about our own claims and more ready to learn from others—not denying that Christ is important to us, not denying that Christ has enriched our lives—but at the same time not being defensive about the fact that others have found other ways that are far more culturally acceptable for them than Christianity might be for them.

James Carroll: Do I think that all religions are equally valid? No, I think there are a lot of charlatans who exploit others' religious yearnings; there are a lot more lies than truth told in the guise of religion. Religion is dangerous. People look to it for wrong things. People are innately superstitious.

Is my attitude such that the Jewish-Christian tradition is the only place where truth resides? Of course not. I'm enough of a conservative to believe that the great religious traditions are all speaking to a valid human experience. We could easily agree on what the great religious traditions are. Beyond that agreement, I'm fairly skeptical. And within those traditions, I'm very skeptical about misused and misappropriated forms.

Harold Kushner: I think different religions can be equally valid in the following way: Different people with the same illness may need different medicines because they're different people. Different people with the same psychological problems sometimes need different kinds of therapy. God affects each of us according to who we are. In that sense, I believe that God is personal. I don't believe that God is an old man with a beard who lives in heaven.

Gravity is impersonal—it treats everyone the same way. Love is personal—I feel something different from what you feel. I respond to one individual differently than another. I believe that God is personal in that way. God affects each of us according to who we are. Some people need the emphasis rendered in Christianity or Hinduism or Buddhism and not in Judaism. There may also be people whose world perspective

> *In the world in which we now live, we must try to live in dialogue with people of other religions. We must try to be more humble about our own claims and more ready to learn from others—not denying that Christ is important to us, not denying that Christ has enriched our lives.*
>
> *Ignacio Castuera*

is precisely Jewish, and the rest of the religions just don't work for them.

In the same way that a doctor will prescribe different medications for the same illness, depending on the patient, yes, in that way, different religions can be valid.

Peggy Way: For me, having a faithful and accurate vision of the world does not mean I can't receive others who have a different vision. In fact, if I have a faithful stance, I don't need to be frightened by others. That's my Christology. What Jesus did on the cross was to receive others even at the point of crucifixion without having to triumph over them. In other words, the response Jesus always gave was to receive others.

Valerie Russell: The Spirit moves in a variety of ways and as a variety of metaphors. I'm not in a position to say if anyone else's religion is valid or not valid—or that God, or whatever you want to call the supreme being, is not a real god.

All religion has to be examined. All religious people need to examine their motivations to see if they are self-seeking, serving their own interests rather than a common good. The demonic can take hold of religious believers very powerfully. We've gotten caught in holy wars. Some would say that the television ministry of the Bakkers and others was a holy war.

We have to sort out what religion holds: Is it freedom and justice and liberation for everyone? Or is it a coronation of the few? In that sense, we have to judge whether our religious beliefs are real or are serving something else.

Mary Gordon: I'm not an ecumenist. I would hate for there to stop being clearly defined doctrinal differences. Those differences represent differences in style, and style expresses who you are.

People who feel passionately enough to define themselves by a religious tradition are going to think that their way is the right way. That's fine. That doesn't bother me. I'm not that way, because my primary definition of myself is not religious. I don't want people to go to the gallows over religion or for there to be inquisitions. I would hope that religion wouldn't cut off conversation.

Probably any person who puts time and energy into a denomination has to think they're doing the right thing, or else why would they be there?

John Vannorsdall: Among the varieties of religious experience and ways of talking about God, one ultimately has to make decisions for oneself. That doesn't mean one person is saying, "I am right and everyone else is wrong." One is saying, "Among these varieties, I make a choice here. This is where I am going to stand. Others have made other choices." Then those others and I, if we so desire, can talk about what that commitment does to each of us. If my religion makes me feel guilty all the time, and this person has a religion that doesn't make him or her feel guilty all the time, then there is a difference and we ought to talk about that. If my way of understanding God allows me to affirm my body and the earth and material things, and the other person's does not, then I would prefer mine. I'm not saying that others are not right in choosing theirs. But we have grounds for conversation. They're not both the same. They do different things. Let's talk about that.

If I'm wandering around in the desert, I'm looking for an oasis. For me, I've found an oasis in the Christian faith. If someone else comes along and says, "Hey, there's another oasis over there," I'm not going to say, "No, this is the only one." I'm going to let them talk about their oasis and maybe I'll even go and see it. But to deny that you personally have found an oasis, and to always be in search of something else, keeps you up in the air with both feet moving, and then you fall down. I like to have one foot planted because I've made some decision, while the other foot is free to move.

James Lawson: We need to become competitive in doing justice and calling the nations of the earth to repentance and peace. I want to insist that whatever differences are among us are not as significant as is the need for dialogue and working together for common purposes. In the twentieth century the earth desperately needs that.

My congregation has been in dialogue with a Jewish synagogue for the last year. While I know the difference, nevertheless I'm committed to the fact that our differences are not so significant as the fact that we're all human beings in the same boat and that unless we work together we will all sink.

I want to insist that whatever differences are among us are not as significant as is the need for dialogue and working together for common purposes. In the twentieth century the earth desperately needs that.

James Lawson

WHAT DOES IT MEAN TO BE FULLY HUMAN?

What Does it Mean to be Fully Human?

Whenever one takes on God's role, one is not being fully human, one is not knowing the limitations of being human.

Peggy Way

Harold Kushner: To be "fully human" is the twentieth-century cliche that paraphrases the biblical image humans have fashioned in the image of God. From over three thousand years of Judaic and biblical tradition and from the wider history of civilization, I've received images of what a real human being looks like. The Yiddish word is "tzaddik," a real person, a person who has fulfilled all the divine potential in himself or herself. He or she has exercised that latent capacity to be good, to be compassionate, loving, responsible —a whole litany of adjectives that make up the image of God.

For me, God is what a human being is at his or her best. God is the omega point that we grow toward.

For me, the fundamental sin is to give up on reaching that potential. Maybe I'm not going to be Isaiah, maybe I'm not going to be Gandhi, but I can be me. And that's a lot more than I am today. For me to say, "Well, it's not worth the trouble," for me to default on realizing any of that potential within me, is the ultimate sin.

Peggy Way: To be fully human must also mean to know *who you are not.* One has to know one's limitations. To be fully human in a religious perspective means to know that one is not God. Whenever one ventures on taking on God's role—whether this is done the way Jim Bakker did it or the way some other theologians do it from a more liberal perspective—whenever one takes on God's role, one is not being fully human, one is not knowing the limitations of being human.

One of those limitations is placed on us by history. We're born into particularity, which brings limitations as well as possibilities. To be fully human and know one's limitations means I have to incorporate my background in some way without hating it.

Ignacio Castuera: For me as a Christian, to be fully human means to express as completely as possible my capacity to care; to understand that I am loved by God and therefore I don't have to react to people in defensive ways. I'm more free to love them.

James Carroll: To be fully human is to be conscious, to be alive to what's happening and what's real, which means, hopefully, to be alive to the playful and delightful and wonderful; to be able to take enormous pleasure in unexpected acts of grace—like that young man who flew an airplane into Red Square. Five thousand Russian radar operators were sitting at their screens waiting all those years for a fleet of enemy B-52s, and here comes this guy flying at 200 feet in a Piper Cub. It boggles the mind. Just at the moment when the American government is trying to demonstrate to the world that Star Wars makes sense, a Piper Cub penetrates the Soviet DEW lines reducing the very notion of their radar barriers to the absurd. Or what does it mean that this disease, AIDS, is stealing love and sex from us and from our young people? We need to be alive to wonderful surprises and awful ones too. Denial is the opposite of consciousness, and denial, whether of AIDS or of the humanity of those Russian radar operators, is what keeps us less than human.

Madeleine L'Engle: To be fully human means to be willing to be alive, and that means being vulnerable. Being vulnerable has become one of those catchwords that has lost its meaning. To be vulnerable means I'm capable of being hurt. The more people I love, the more I'm open to being hurt. To get married is a vulnerable act. To have children or to have friends is part of the risk-taking we have to do if we're to be creative and if our humanness is to be furthered.

I don't think we're human. I think we're potentially human. Jesus came and showed us what it is to be human, and we were so terrified of it that we crucified it. We still do that.

We're afraid to be human because if we're human we might get hurt. We live in a society that tells us to "Take aspirin, Anacin"—so there's no pain, whatever we do. We don't grow if we're not open to hurt.

William Sloane Coffin: What we're called to do in this world is to become vulnerable. The greatest thing in grief is that you're vulnerable. The greatest thing when you're madly in love is that you're vulnerable. You're

We're afraid to be human because if we're human we might get hurt.

Madeleine L'Engle

aware of feelings and thoughts that you don't have in normal daily living.

There's a certain truth about the statement, "There are no atheists in foxholes." In foxholes you're living at a more profound depth than you usually live. You're more vulnerable. More things are exchanged between two men in a foxhole within an hour than most people care to share with someone else in a lifetime. That is the kind of vulnerabilty I implore people to accept.

I hate *machismo*. It steels you from the very thing you need to be available to. For instance, one thing that a cold fist can't accept is a helping hand. We need to do away with all *machismo* and learn from women what vulnerability is all about.

The woman most in need of liberation is the woman in every man. The man most in need of liberation, obviously, is the man in every woman. It's this kind of tenderness, of vulnerability, of openness to something new, to experiences more awesome, more wonderful, or more meaningful than what we know on a daily basis, that's what religion is really all about.

Will Campbell: The words "fully human" mean "fully free." In my sixty-three years on this planet, the one thing I've tried to do the most is survive as a human being. That's a dangerous and radical undertaking, because there are all these impositions, all these institutions, all of which are after my soul. Education, religion, politics—all institutions are after my soul. To be fully human is to be free.

To be fully human is to be free.

Will Campbell

WHAT MATTERS, ANYWAY?

□

T. George Harris: The question of meaning has been the obsession of all of us, whether there is an essence for living. Is there a reason for getting up in the morning?

Asking questions like, "Did I break a rule today?" "Am I liked by others because I followed the rules?" are not the essential questions for today's generation.

The essential questions are: "Why am I here?" "Can I love?" "Does it matter?" "What is worth dying for?" Dying is not that hard, but dying is hard if there's nothing worth dying for.

Daniel Matthews: Loving relationships give my life meaning. I live to love and be loved. I work hard to win affection and approval. If I'm really honest, what I deeply want is to be loved. I want to find someone who will accept my love, whether it's on the street, in the elevator, or within my family. I desperately want to love and be loved. When I feel like I'm loved, everything seems to make sense.

Mary Gordon: I've never felt the temptation of meaninglessness, so I can't answer the question directly. I've always thought my life had meaning because I've always had work and love. On the whole, I've found life very interesting, particularly in regard to my responses to suffering. God or religion certainly do not give my life meaning. My life is meaningful because I can have relationships with human beings and have my work.

James Lawson: The unity I feel in my own life, the well-being and sense of belonging that give my life meaning, of being "meant to be," comes mostly from being birthed in a Methodist parsonage where there was a lot of love—and where, in time, I recognized that that love was indeed the power by which I could creatively deal with racism and violence in the world.

Valerie Russell: What gives my life meaning is love. None of us is meant to go through this journey alone. We who are blessed have people who support us and love us, whether through blood lines, marriage, or some other sense of covenant which is extended family. That love and support are dynamic and create meaning.

Ignacio Castuera: What gives my life meaning is struggle and knowing that God is present in struggle. To search for meaning as an end in itself takes me away from the daily struggles of life. The ability to stand up and address different issues, to care profoundly for what happens in places I've never visited—all of these actions come from the idea that God cares and people care and are struggling to communicate God's concern. Such realizations really turn me on. I could be philosophical about it, but this is what it boils down to.

Valerie Russell: Without a faith in God and a feeling of empowerment by a spirit that undergirds us and filters through us, we wouldn't be able to do half of what we do. There are days I wouldn't get up in the morning if I weren't a person of faith who believes that there is a creative energy in the universe that struggles through me and with me and will struggle long after I die. I do what I can everyday to be a good person and help others who want to be humane. It takes faith to respond this way. We should do what we can, but we don't have to do everything because the struggle has been here before us and will be here after us.

Harold Kushner: The time when my faith in God's providence was most tested was when my wife and I learned that our son was going to die of an uncurable disease. This was not the way the world was supposed to work. Here was an innocent child from probably the most religiously committed family in town—this wasn't supposed to be happening to him.

I questioned whether life was worthwhile, whether there was any purpose for being a good, honest, religious person. It's the question of Ecclesiastes: "If I'm good and my neighbor is bad, if I'm honest and he's not, if I'm caring and he's selfish, and we both grow old and die the same way, what is the purpose of being good?" Those questions challenged my faith.

What gives my life meaning is struggle and knowing that God is present in struggle.

Ignacio Castuera

45

But I came to affirm the worthwhileness of life because of my outrage. "If life is meaningless, why does it hurt so much to know that my child will die in adolescence?" I asked myself on more than one occasion. "If life is meaningless, I ought to be able to dismiss this and say, 'Easy come, easy go,' like a fly or insect dying." I came to realize that life was worthwhile because I felt so much pain.

I find myself still forced to go back and doubt. For example, when I've worked hard for interfaith/interracial understanding, for world peace, for a sense of honesty and decency and unselfishness among my congregants, and I don't make a lot of difference, I ask myself, "To what end have I labored? Why do I knock myself out so much when it doesn't make a difference?"

"What makes human beings so different from other species?" provides the answer to its own question. What makes us different is that we ask "What makes us different?" We can't settle for just existing. There's something special in every one of us that affirms the preciousness of life. When I wonder "Does it really make any difference if I live?"—"Does God care?" out of that inner voice, I get my response which silences my doubts.

John Vannorsdall: Believing in God means that the world and I have a future, that it's not all random or futility. It's not foreordained that we'll always have war, hunger, poverty, and injustice, that children are abused, or that husbands strike their wives.

What sustains me is the belief that God is. And because God is, we have a future that is different from the present which I know. Peter Berger has said, "The rumors of angels that I hear about are ultimately going to be more than rumors." The peace that the Bible promises will come to pass.

As long as I have this assurance, I'm able to get up in the morning and face the hardships I have to face.

Will Campbell: What gives my life meaning is life. It's a gas! I like it. That comment could be expounded, but I don't know what else to say. Life is good.

*W*hat sustains me is the belief that God is. And because God is, we have a future that is different from the present I know.

John Vannorsdall

WHO IS JESUS?

James Forbes: Who is Jesus? Jesus is my friend. I like Jesus. He was a very "together" person. I like his freedom to be himself and to be for others. I like his capacity to keep pace with his own sense of who he was and the destiny he believed he was called to fulfill. I like his willingness to suffer for things he believed in. I like the evidence I get that the God of the universe honored him because he was faithful to what he was about.

Jesus is the one from whom I get clues as to what the good life is about. Jesus is the one who's invited me to get with it. If I can stand the pressure and bear the cross, it'll be a fruitful enterprise. We will make a difference in the world together.

Jesus is also the one in whom I find the invitation to wholeness, a clue to forgiveness for my sins, as well as the promise that I can live a life that increasingly honors God and loves community and serves the world—rather than being a person who continues to spoil the dream of the creator.

Dan Wakefield: I think of the historical figure as Jesus. And then I think of Christ as the Spirit still with us, and I think of that as light and a creative force.

Rosemary Radford Ruether: Jesus was a first-century Jew. We need to start there because a lot of our definitions try to deny that. Jesus was a first-century messianic Jew who announced the kingdom of God and understood himself to be a messianic prophet to fellow Jews. I don't think Jesus intended to found a Christian church. The Christian church happened. His understanding of the kingdom was that of "good news to the poor" and of risking oneself to offer God's unconditional love to those who were most despised and left out of the religious system of his time.

I see us relating to Jesus as the Christ essentially by relating to that kind of message and life style. He becomes Christ in that context. That's what redemptive life is all about—living in that way.

Robert McAfee Brown: Imagine a religious leader today taking someone from the Internal Revenue Service on his team. It boggles the mind. The

Imagine a religious leader today taking someone from the Internal Revenue Service on his team. It boggles the mind.

Robert McAfee Brown

people of Jesus' day knew him as a fellow human being who got tired and hungry, and even on one occasion got so discouraged he burst into tears. He transformed their lives.

When talking about who Jesus was, the people of his time realized that human categories weren't sufficient. God was present in a special way and all kinds of titles emerged: Messiah, Savior, Lord, probably forty or fifty different titles. But the point is that those titles came as a result of their experience dealing with this human life. They had to employ language to describe Jesus that gave him a special quality because they saw God present in a human life to a degree that they didn't see in anybody else.

Jesus is the one who never forgot that he and the sacred Source were one.

Virginia Mollenkott

Harold Kushner: Who is Jesus for me? Wouldn't it be great if right here on television I accepted Jesus as Lord? Imagine what that would do for the ratings.

For me objectively as a Jew, Jesus was a first-century patriot who taught things that were within the parameters of Jewish theology at that time, even if they were somewhat controversial. He was a striking teacher and marvelously effective in communicating his embodiment of values held by most Jews of the first century.

But I can't stop there. Jesus for me is the central figure worshiped by my Christian friends and neighbors, and I have to respect him as their Savior even if he doesn't play that role for me. As such, he becomes an instrument through which my God, the God of the Hebrew Bible, becomes the universal God—the God not only of Christians, but the God whose impact is not limited to a single nation. This, I have to believe, is what God wanted in the beginning.

God's original charge to the Jewish people was to make the whole world conscious of God's moral demands. Jesus becomes a Jewish instrument of doing this. More significantly, through the story of the passion, crucifixion, and resurrection, he comes to embody the idea of a God who doesn't always control events, a God who suffers and shares with us human vulnerability, and triumphs over vulnerability. The cross is a profoundly religious symbol, which conveys the idea that suffering and death do not have to be the end, and you don't measure the success of life either by its length or wealth.

Virginia Mollenkott: Jesus made it all possible. Jesus is my Savior in the sense of making it all possible. Jesus is the one who never forgot that he and the sacred Source were one. That's what I'm trying to remember: that I and my sacred Source are also one. Jesus talked about not speaking his own words, but speaking the words of the one who sent him. He prayed that we all would know that oneness that he felt with the Source. Human cruelty stems from forgetting who we are. We are intended to treat each other lovingly, with respect, and cherish the image of God in each other.

Martin Marty: Scholar James D. G. Dunn ran the whole scriptures through a computer (*The Mind of James D. G. Dunn*) and came up with a phrase, "The early Christian church was not united. It was very divided: Jew *or* Greek, male *or* female, slave *or* free, *or* all one in Christ." The church sure doesn't seem to act like they're one in Christ. Is the Bible only for bishops or only for elders or only for congregations? No, it's for everyone.

Everything they said about Jesus the Christ comes down to the formula that the human Jesus is the exalted Lord. All would agree to that statement somehow. That statement is the minimum and maximum of what I can say. If I skip the emphasis of Jesus' humanity, then I don't have a context of God as Christian. If he's not the exalted Lord, but just somebody who gives me freedom—well, I get that from Thomas Jefferson more sufficiently. The two perspectives have to merge. That's the heart of the Christian proclamation.

Walter Wink: I don't think of Jesus as perfect in the sense that I try to be perfect in my own life. I think of Jesus as whole. If you're perfect, you have to be flawless. When I think of someone who's whole, I think of someone who's incorporated all of his or her own shadow—one's darkness and sin and lust and anger and violence—raised it to consciousness, and offered it to God as a part of the fullness of being human—and finding that it has been transformed. I think of Jesus as whole in this sense.

Jesus was so adamant about being faithful to who he was. He became the best Jesus that he could become.

Ada Maria Isasi-Diaz

Jesus is the vision of what it means to be a whole person, to be a fully human being. When the scriptures speak of Jesus as the Son of God, I understand it to mean that Jesus shows us what it means to be fully human and to incarnate God fully in human life. God wants that for all of us. God wants to be alive in my body; God wants to be able to act through my body and speak through my mouth. Jesus did this and we're all able to do it to some degree. Jesus shows me what it would mean to live this kind of life.

Ada Maria Isasi-Diaz: The issue of the divinity of Jesus is extremely complex. What does it mean to be divine? I come from a church in which every time Mass is celebrated, when the priest mingles the water into the wine, he says, addressing Jesus Christ, "May we become participants in your divinity, you who became participant in our humanity."

Was Jesus divine? Yes, I believe Jesus was divine. But there's also an element of the divine in all of us. The church teaches that we participate in the divine.

Jesus was so adamant about being faithful to who he was. He was able to become the best Jesus that he could become. I think that is a great part of what we mean when we say he was divine. In that sense, his participation in the divine means "fullness of being."

You and I hopefully are trying to become the best person we can be. Becoming the best Ada Maria I can be means participating in the divine. I don't try to do things the way Jesus did them because I'm not Jesus and I'm not called to do things the way Jesus did them. But I do try to imitate Jesus' depth of commitment and willingness to go all the way, to become fully himself.

Bernie Siegel: Woody Allen said, "Jesus was a very well-adjusted only child." Jesus is a teacher, which is probably the best thing I could say about him. He was both a literal and metaphorical individual who chose to do something and live a certain way to teach us that we don't have to be crucified more than once. I see people who have multiple crucifixions and never choose to get resurrected. I try to teach them that they are lovable and are entitled to resurrection and new life. Jesus' path and pattern is an example we all can follow and learn from.

Is it literally possible that it could have been a virgin birth? That type of question also fascinates me. If we can make cancer go away, if we can heal a disease, why not biblical miracles? Could all this happen? My answer as a scientist and physician is "Sure." But that's not the important issue, whether the virgin birth literally happened or not. His teaching is what is important, not so much how he was created.

We're all capable of what Jesus achieved and accomplished in the world today. It's easy to become a monk and sit in a cave and say, "I will love." Fine. But we all find it hard to live with someone who snores. I say, get out of that cave and live with someone who snores. If you can still be loving while living with someone who snores, then you've accomplished something.

John Spong: Jesus is the place I look to, to try to understand the reality of God as best as I'm capable of understanding. When I talk to Jews and ask them where they look, they tell me it's the Torah. Buddhists tell me it's the enlightened Buddha. When I talk to Islamic people, to some degree it's the prophet Muhammad.

Every religious tradition has a point of reference where the divine and human come together in an understandable way. Jesus is that for me. That's a unique claim that I make for Jesus, but I make it unique only subjectively. Jesus is the place where *I* meet God. I don't believe Jesus is the place necessarily where every other human being must meet God, because I think God is bigger than my understanding, my religious system, my tradition.

Roy Sano: I have to take very seriously the fact that he is a very different person from myself in a number of ways. This is a part of my faith that I've increasingly taken more earnestly as a result of being bicultural. There was a time when I used to ask, "How can I be Christian and yet Buddhist?" My Japanese culture is still a part of me. But now I'm beginning to ask, "How can I be Christian without being Buddhist?" I have to be aware of distinctions and how I have to bring them together.

What attracts me to Jesus is his capacity to relate to people who are different from him. As a Jewish male, he is particularly remembered for how he related to women. He also related to people in power as well as to the desperately poor. Although he was Jewish, he related to people who were a symbol of a mixture of race, the Samaritans. That's important to my wife and me because she is a child of cross-racial marriage. But it's also important when it comes to gender. We are uncomfortable with people who do not meekly stay within their gender role.

Harvey Cox: Jesus is the figure who prevents me from falling into despair about the possibility of humans. When I'm tempted to say, "This is a fluke, a bad joke evolution has played on us," I see Jesus as able to show that humans can be what God intended humans to be.

My translation of Jesus is an AIDS patient or a homeless person.

Daniel Berrigan

Daniel Berrigan: My translation of Jesus is an AIDS patient or a homeless person. I don't think I'm very romantic about this notion. This is where my faith hits ground and hits suffering. Either Jesus is presenting himself in these types of people, or the whole thing is a mime show and the book is closed. But I don't think it is.

Carmen Guerrero: As Christians we believe Jesus to be the Son of God, the anointed one, the Messiah, the one God sent to be in our midst. I think of Jesus as my friend. I believe the statement in our faith about his being the Son of God. When I think in terms of being friends with the God of the universe, sometimes it's more than I can handle. For me, a friend is more than a casual acquaintance. A friend is someone for whom I would die. Jesus loves me so much that he would die for me—and did.

Desmond Tutu: Jesus is one who makes God real. The wonderful stories that he tells have made me realize more and more that I'm all gift and that I have a God who reckons that I count. I count so much that God gave the very best that he could, the life of Jesus for me.

Jesus could weep. Sometimes when you look at the ugliness that make's you weep, you know that the heart of God is also weeping. Jesus is for real. He does not give up on anyone, least of all on me.

WHAT'S THE USE OF THE BIBLE?

Will Campbell: No one believes the Bible literally, no one. For instance, I asked a fellow visiting my part of the country (Tennessee), "Brother, do you believe the Bible literally?" And he said, "Yes, sir!" "Word for word, just as it is written?" I asked. "Yes, sir!" he replied enthusiastically. "Word for word! And there are ten million people in this country who believe it literally."

"Fantastic!" I said. "I do too. I didn't know anybody else in the world agreed with me. I've got this project in west Nashville I'd like to get you involved with. Jesus said he came to open the doors of prisons and let prisoners free. Now I can't tear a prison down by myself. But you say you believe the Bible literally and that ten million other people in this country believe it literally, so together we can demolish some prisons and set those prisoners free. Let's do it."

"Wait a minute," he said. "What Jesus meant by that statement was …."

I interrupted. "You said you believed the Bible literally, 'word for word,' and that is literally what Jesus and Isaiah both said. Now are you going to help me or not?" I asked. Well, the prison is still standing.

Nobody believes the Bible literally. But to me it is the source of religious truth if we accept it for what it is: a book about who God is and about who we are as humans.

John Spong: The Bible has been ruined for most religious people by the kind of superstition we have placed on it. As a child, I remember that a Bible was set on a coffee table in our living room, and if anyone dared put a glass of milk or Coca-Cola on the Bible, he or she was reprimanded because it was a holy book.

We've printed Bibles in the format of dictionaries and encyclopedias to make sure no one reads them. They're not "user-friendly." Almost no one picks up those types of books just to read them. We've printed Bibles on tissue-thin paper with a lot of hieroglyphics all over the pages. So we don't encourage Bible reading, and that's a tragedy.

Jim Wallis: For me the Bible is central, although there are many arguments about how literally we should interpret it. But that's not really our problem.

Our problem is that we don't take it (the Bible) seriously enough, including all the fundamentalists who claim to.

Jim Wallis

Our problem is that we don't take it seriously enough, including all the fundamentalists who claim to.

In the biblical world view you don't *know* something until it changes your life. Head knowledge isn't the end of the process. To *believe* the Bible means *becoming* biblical people, to begin to live what the Bible is telling us. Knowing the Bible this way overturns everything we want to believe about ourselves: our comfortable assumptions, our systems, our structures. The Bible turns all that upside down and places our feet on the path.

Harold Kushner: The Bible is the basis of my Jewish tradition and my own personal faith system. We Jews are a people who elevate study to the level of a religious deed. We worship God through studying the Bible. It's at the heart of our services and our personal discipline.

I take the Bible seriously, even if not literally. To take it literally I'd the people who wrote it down never made a mistake, that the people who copied it never made a mistake, and the people who taught us to understand it never made a mistake. That's a lot to buy into.

So I take it very seriously as the record of God's revelation, the record of a people coming into the presence of God and understanding something about how they were meant to live that human beings had never understood before.

There are times when I'm troubled by what I read in the Bible: the command to "wipe out every last Amalekite man, woman, and child," or to "burn down the altars of the Canaanites," or passages that seem to take women's lives less seriously then men's. All of that bothers me because the Bible has taught me something about the dignity of every human being and about the sanctity of life. It's not that my modern sensibility is passing judgment on the Bible.

I'm calling the Bible to witness against itself. There are other passages in the Bible that trouble me too, such as in Deuteronomy where it says, "If you live a good life, you'll be rewarded; and if you stray from these paths, you'll be punished." I've had to acknowledge that the world doesn't work like that. The Bible has to talk that way not because it's the only way God knows how to speak, but because the Bible was addressed to a nation in its infancy, to the Israelites three thousand years ago, who were first learning how the world works. Just as you talk to a child differently from the way you talk to an adult about right and wrong, the Bible is God's first word, not God's last.

I read the Bible historically, through thousands of years of Jewish interpretation, which tells me, for example, to take "Love the stranger as yourself" and "Don't bear a grudge" from Leviticus 19:34 more seriously than the passage about killing the Amalekites. "An eye for an eye" is not meant to be taken literally, but is a statement about justice. It means to punish criminals in accordance with what they've done—neither more nor less than what they deserve.

Rosemary Radford Ruether: Jewish and Christian traditions use scripture differently. First of all, Jews don't accept the New Testament, and

Christians, although they pretend to accept the whole scripture, in fact don't accept much of the Old Testament. For example, they throw out the entire Levitical codes. We actually have a *selective* canon which we use as authoritative and foundational for our continual reflection in historical tradition. But it's also an ambivalent line of collective wisdom. The Bible is full of acts we have to question, things like sexism and violence and the condoning of slavery.

We have to evaluate that foundation just as the early Christians themselves had to, and then decide again and again what is the authoritative component of it all and what is a distortion of human sinfulness.

Nobody simply takes the whole scripture as a total authority. They may pretend to, but as soon as you ask them, "Why is it that you don't take the Levitical codes as authoritative?" they have no answer. Because, of course, they inherit a tradition of almost two thousand years of Christianity that has rejected those codes. We live in a community of tradition that is continually reevaluating what is authoritative. Each of us as an individual has to come to terms with it ourselves if we are to have an authentic selfhood and an authentic relationship to that tradition.

People have been bullied by clergy and "experts" and biblical scholars into thinking they're not capable of interpreting scripture.

Walter Wink

Ada Maria Isasi-Diaz: Being Roman Catholic, of course, I hardly knew the Bible until recently. We started reading it mainly after Vatican II in the mid 1960s. Before then the Catholic Church for centuries conveyed to the laity that they were not educated enough to read the Bible, that priests and the hierarchy of the church should read it and then interpret it for the people. For centuries, ordinary Roman Catholics did not read the Bible, and that's still true for the older generation.

As a child of the sixties, I have talked to my parents and aunts and uncles about why they should read the Bible. Their response has been, "No, no, that just confuses us." They know about the Bible from what their priest taught them and nothing else.

Now, after Vatican II, there is a whole change of attitude encouraging Catholics to study the Bible. But we just can't change people's attitudes that quickly when a certain outlook has prevailed for centuries. Personally

I don't know that I can say scripture holds "X, Y, or Z" authority for me. Scripture is one of several elements that shapes my beliefs and helps me to know what I should do, where I must go.

Walter Wink: My task is primarily to ask questions, to help people see in the text new possibilities for interpretation. It's a lot of fun teaching this way because people have been bullied by clergy and "experts" and biblical scholars into thinking they're not capable of interpreting scripture. One of the attitudes I want my students to recover is a sense of their own power to be interpreters, that they have the capacity to hear God speak to them directly through scripture and directly through others in their Bible study class.

As a leader, I don't see it as my task to tell people what they should believe about the Bible. Rather, my role is to help them discover truth and meaning from the Bible themselves. When that happens, various truths emerge and people realize there are many right answers to a really good question; really good questions are inexhaustible in stirring up new answers. This type of thinking frees people from a wooden sense of authority about scripture, as if there's only one correct answer, or the answer is in the back of the book.

Virginia Mollenkott: The Bible still holds a great deal of authority for me. I check everything out scripturally.

When I was in my thirties, I had a terrific shock: I was reading a feminist author who claimed there were two versions of creation in the Book of Genesis. I had read Genesis frequently since age four, but I had never noticed two versions of creation. So I dived for my Bible, and lo and behold, there were two versions of creation. In one, Adam was created first and then all the animals and then Eve. In the other version, Adam and Eve were created together on the sixth day after all the animals were created. Imagine my shock! Here were two different plots.

At the time I had a Ph.D. in English literature and was a specialist on John Milton and was teaching people how to read carefully. "What is wrong with me?" I asked myself.

If we don't rescue the essence of biblical truth from cultural norms, we're going to lose the Bible.

John Spong

I realized I had been reading through an interpretive grid, as everyone does. My grid said there are no contradictions in the Bible, which is also the fundamentalist grid. So I couldn't see two versions because it felt like a contradiction. Later I came to understand it as two emphases.

But that experience taught me the importance of hermeneutics. I began to see that if I really believe what I say—that the Bible is the word of God—then I ought to read with more care, not less, than I read anything else.

So I began to read the Bible and to apply all the reading techniques I had learned during my doctoral studies, which I had never applied before because of my fundamentalist grid. Everything looked different then.

When you read in context, you pay attention to figures of speech, historical content, literary content, whether what you're reading is poetry or analysis or narrative. It makes a tremendous difference.

The norm to interpret the Bible is, "Is this life-giving for us?" "Good news" means good news.

Hyung Kyung Chung

John Spong: We think the tenth commandment says, "You shall not covet." But that's not what it says. When you read it in Exodus 20, it says, "You shall not covet . . . your neighbor's wife." What does that mean? (There's nowhere in the Bible where it tells us not to covet our neighbor's husband, so presumably that's okay.) The truth is, the Bible was written only for men, because women were property and were not considered part of the covenant community (nor were they the audience for whom the Ten Commandments was written). If you don't believe this, all you have to do is read the rest of that commandment. What it really says is, "You shall not covet your neighbor's wife, nor his ox, nor his ass, nor anything that is your neighbor's." That was the way people thought of women—as pieces of property.

The commandment about adultery was written during a time when polygamy, not monogamy, was the style of life. Three hundred years after the Ten Commandments were written, Solomon had a thousand wives. What does adultery mean if you have a thousand wives? If you've got a thousand wives and still are tempted to commit adultery, I think you've got a problem.

So much of the Bible is written in terms of cultural norms that if we don't rescue the essence of biblical truth from those norms, we're going to lose the Bible. I can't buy into those cultural norms.

Hyung Kyung Chung: I will only have power when we as women interpret the Bible as a life-giving word. In the past, the Bible has been used against Asian women to justify abuse. I had a serious struggle with the Bible when I found out that Western men had decided together what was the *canon* and what was not. For instance, they rejected the Gospel of Mary which is more woman-oriented. Today's Bible was compiled by Western men who lived in the Western world two thousand years ago and didn't know me or my people's struggles or our stories for liberation and survival.

The Bible only has power when we interpret it as life-giving. The Bible is a reference, a context for my people which *we* use for inspiration and wisdom. It is a reference for us, and we are the text. The Bible doesn't give us all the answers, like how to prevent a nuclear war, how to deal with issues of battered women, or whether America should intervene in Asian countries. The Bible doesn't say anything specifically about these modern issues we are struggling with.

The norm for interpreting the Bible is to ask, "Is this life-giving for us, or is it death-giving?" "Good news" means *good news.*

Elisabeth Schüssler Fiorenza: We need to think of the Bible as a prototype, the first type, which set Christian life and community in motion, but which does not need to be repeated. It needs to be worked with and therefore articulated in every new situation.

For me, the authority of the Bible is given into the hands of people struggling to live the Christian vision, struggling against oppression and dehumanization, especially of women. The experience of the presence of God in this struggle then helps us discern which texts liberate or oppress. And we can't say it once for all. A text like "God is love" or "Love your neighbor" can be very liberating. But then if you counsel a battered woman and use those texts to justify her staying within her violent marriage relationship, that makes the texts oppressive rather than liberating.

Clarice Martin: One reason we have so many denominations is because of hermeneutics. Some believing communities have decided that particular traditions are binding and some aren't. Ultimately, answers are decided within communities of faith. A pertinent example of this for me as an African American is the slave injunction. Paul says, "Slaves should be submissive to masters," but there came a time in the church when we decided that this verse about slavery should no longer be binding. Of course, there were communities of faith that disagreed with this new consensus about slavery in the nineteenth century, but the majority agreed that slavery was inconsistent with the overarching will of God for humanity. In this example, we see how consensus also is a factor in determining what is normative and binding for us.

James Carroll: It's important to remember that the Bible is not God, just as the church is not God. God is God. For me, the Bible has the same authority, more or less, that the earth has. It points beyond itself to God and puts me in the presence of another essence that is a relevant authority. And it's important because it has been the life experience and authority of my people, of Jews and Christians for thousands of years. It's an elegant, powerful, wonderfully literate distillation.

The Bible talks *about* God, and talking about God is one of the most important things we can do. If we don't find a way to talk about God, we substitute wrong things in place of God—as humans often do. For example, in our culture the god we have is security, which is the opposite of letting go and trusting. Seeking security drives us nuts as homeowners because of our volatile economy, and for years it drove us nuts as Americans because of the cold war. Our need for security is a kind of god. If we talk about God as Jews and Christians, then we learn not to make the wrong things into God.

Madeleine L'Engle: The Bible is true. It's not entirely factual, but it's true. That's hard for a lot of people to understand. Fact and truth are not the same. I love what Karl Barth said: "I take the Bible far too seriously to take it literally."

We Jews have seen the Torah as not just a book of stories or law codes, but as a love letter from God.

Harold Kushner

Some of the Bible is history and some of the Bible is story, and we don't always know which is which. But it doesn't matter. What I'm looking for in the Bible is truth.

If you look at the great protagonists in the Old and New Testaments, not one of them is qualified to do what God is asking that individual to do. (In a sense we're all unqualified.) God goes to great pains to pick the unqualified. If you were starting a nation, would you pick a woman past menopause and a man a hundred years old? That doesn't seem sensible, but that's what God did.

The message is clear. If you think you're qualified, you might believe you did a good job. If you know you're unqualified, you realize you can only accomplish because somehow you're empowered by God.

Harold Kushner: I read the Torah as Jews have read it and loved it for centuries. For example, I can tell you what is the middle word in the Torah. I can tell you what is the middle letter in the Torah. Over the generations Jewish scholars have read the Torah not as a novel to see how it ends, but as a love letter. For instance, "Why did he use this word instead of that word?" "Why is there a space here?" "Why a comma here instead of a period?" That's the way you read a love letter and wonder, "What did he or she mean by this word?" We Jews have seen the Torah as not just a book of stories or law codes, but as a love letter from God.

WHO'S GOT THE TRUTH?

James Forbes: From where I stand, this is the way *I* see it. But others who stand somewhere else, see it differently and might disagree with me over an issue which they obviously believe is the right way. "Do I have a direct line on truth because it's *my* perspective?" Is my standpoint such that God says, "That's really it?"

Every religious person should frequently ask, "From this limited place where I am, how accurate is my vision of reality?" which gives me space to ask others to do the same about their perspective.

I do not have any sense that my limited mind encompasses the totality of truth. *My* religious documents, *my* religious principles, cannot boast of being the end of wisdom God revealed to humankind. No one should claim absolute rightness for his or her own limited perspective.

Martin Marty: At the turn of the century, there was a cartoon character created by a man named Mr. Dooley in Chicago. This cartoon character once was featured as saying, "The fanatic is the person who know's he doing exactly what the Lord would do if God were also in possession of the facts." Are you and I also fanatics who think we're doing what the Lord would do if God were also in possession of the facts? Do we know something God doesn't know?

We need to remain engaged in dialogue with those who differ from us even though we may never agree on details of faith. I'm not a fundamentalist, but I can't disregard fundamentalism. I'm not Eastern Orthodox, yet they're witnessing to elements of the faith I'd miss if they weren't here.

John Spong: I'm quite willing for anyone to demonstrate to me that my beliefs and values are inadequate. I'm constantly changing my views.

I grew up as a fundamentalist in the South. I was a racist, a male chauvinist, and a homophobic personality. Gradually I've realized that I'm called to shed some of those prejudices.

I don't have any difficulty with people who are willing to scrutinize their values and beliefs. But what I've found in a lot of religious people is that they're not willing to debate, examine, or even share their beliefs for the sake of learning or having them nuanced.

That's because they don't really believe. They believe in believing. There's a big difference. Their belief in believing is what gives them personal security. When someone challenges their opinions, they respond with emotional hostility.

For me personally, any time my beliefs are challenged and I respond angrily, I demonstrate that I don't really hold fast to those beliefs at all, but I need them desperately for my own psyche's sake.

Carmen Guerrero: One of the things we can do is respect others who differ from us and not be insistent that everyone be like us. We could be wrong. If everyone is like us, there's no opportunity for other possibilities. Mutual respect is vital. We need to listen to each other and engage in the possibility that other people have something to offer us.

Harvey Cox: I've been accused of seeking out people who differ with me and reveling in finding some common ground or usefulness between us. I have an underlying confidence that even though we disagree, in the end our efforts in seeking truth are going to be pointing in the same direction.

Daniel Berrigan: Let's see where the differences are, and if they seem to be intractable, let's rejoice in that.

All of our work in social justice from the beginning of the civil rights movement has been ecumenical and encompassed a peaceable group of people who agreed on not wanting certain laws, such as allowing murder, to be legal. We vulnerably work together even though we come from all sorts of different religious backgrounds. The differences tend to be mitigated, not resolved, in practice. When we see someone in danger, at least we can utter a common outcry.

Will Campbell: Last year I was involved in a conference called "Life Issues." We convened people who were very active in the "right to life" issue but who favored the death penalty. We also convened people who

We need to engage in the possibility that the other person has something to offer us.

Carmen Guerrero

were working hard on abolishing the death penalty but who were "pro-choice" on abortion. We convened people who were working hard to stop nuclear proliferation.

In my judgment, and I reserve the right to be wrong about everything including this statement, those three groups are at least "kissing cousins." But frequently we won't acknowledge any common mutuality. We talk about one specific issue with one specific group, but not the other group, such as abortion, but won't talk about the death penalty; or we talk about nuclear proliferation, but won't talk about abortion. These three groups need to begin at least speaking to one another.

Roy Sano: We bicker and backbite, and that's reality. The backbiting is vicious. Instead, we need to dialogue. I look for chances to have these types of conversation. We have them in my denomination.

It's better to keep talking *with* each other, rather than *about* each other or *at* each other. It's important to set up these dialogues so people realize that discussion is important and needs to happen among us.

Hyung Kyung Chung: When I think about the urgency of survival of the humanity and of this earth, religious solidarity seems more important than religious dialogue. When I have to fight with people from other faiths (which happens only when others hurt and oppress me and my people), it's because I've challenged their belief system and its consequences. If others don't actively hurt my people's survival and liberation, then I genuinely want to learn from those who differ with me and enhance my small way of understanding God. I want to be open to other revelations of God so my perspective can be enlarged and enriched by their perspective. God is so big.

Delores Williams: I'm not closed to the idea that God is manifested in a variety of cultures and ways, and those different ways are just as credible as the ways I believe that God is manifested in my world. For instance, what Muslims believe is just as credible as what I believe, which is derived from the black Judeo-Christian tradition.

It's better to keep talking with each other rather than about each other or at each other.

Roy Sano

Harvey Cox: I've had lots and lots of experience with interfaith dialogue, and I've begun finding that the Hindu or Muslim partner was saying, "Now that we've had this preliminary chit-chat, what about Jesus?" They have their own convictions, but they want to hear about Jesus and know what I *honestly* believe about him.

We're entering a period in Christian theology, even in Christian faith, in which we can't assume that what the Hindu or Muslim thinks about Jesus can be totally excluded from our understanding as Christians about who we think Jesus was. We don't have a monopoly on defining the meaning of Jesus.

If there was ever any proof of this, it's in the life of Mahatma Gandhi. He insisted that he was a Hindu, and he remained one his entire life; yet he said the most important document he'd ever read was the Sermon on the Mount. The person whose life appealed to him more than anyone else was Jesus.

I began finding that the Hindu or Muslim partner was saying, "Now that we've had this preliminary chit-chat, what about Jesus?"

Harvey Cox

John Spong: The Hindus have as many variations as we have of Christians. We call them denominations. Even though the Hindus don't get that formal, their variations are as extreme as our denominations are. They have simple-minded, noneducated, illiterate Indian folk whose Hindu religion is manipulative and superstitious to a fault. They also have incredibly abstract, brilliant-thinking philosophers.

One element missing in the Hindu tradition that is so present in Christianity is a willingness to judge other people as inadequate. For instance, the Hindu philosopher would look at the superstitious, illiterate Hindu and not believe that this person is wrong or ignorant or inept. The philosopher would believe that the superstitious person is responding to as much of God as he or she can experience. The simple-minded Hindu is embracing as much of God as his or her consciousness in its present state of development can embrace. Everyone would rejoice in each varied religious outlook. If anyone tried to change another's faith, it would not be to challenge the beliefs of an individual on content, but rather to begin a relationship that has the potential for raising each person's level of consciousness to grasp a bigger picture of truth.

*Truth has a
self-authenticating
quality about it.
When someone
resonates truth,
we respond.*

Desmond Tutu

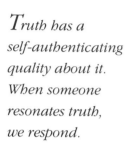

I'd like more nonjudgmental attitudes like those of the Hindus in the Christian church, instead of having religious fights or consigning people to hell or writing letters and telling someone he is "the devil incarnate" because he disagrees with a certain point of view. We have a lot to learn from Hindus in this area.

Desmond Tutu: I'm a traditionalist. Yet I'm also quite awe-struck when I hear new ideas from brilliant theologians and scientists that help clarify my framework of truth.

Truth has a self-authenticating quality about it. When someone resonates truth, we respond. Why is it that even those who aren't Christian, even those who are atheists will recognize Mother Teresa as a good person and say she is a "saint"? When you ask them what they mean by such a description, they can't quite explain their terminology, but they recognize a good person.

In the end, you discover truth has a certain ring about it.

Martin Marty: God is perceived as a being who loves all and relies on us to exemplify and spread "the word" even though a vast majority are not going to convert. I don't care how romantic a missionary organization is—we're not going to get fervent people of other faiths to convert to Christianity very often.

This call to spread the gospel makes us dependent upon God. It means that if faith in Christ is an enhancement to my life, I'm going to share it with a person who asks about it. I'm not going to have a Jewish-Christian dialogue in order to pounce on someone else who differs with me and testify that he or she had "better convert." That type of behavior denies the purpose of the dialogue, is destructive, and is not what conversion is all about.

If I have a word processor I really like, I tell people about it. If I am on a diet or exercise regimen I like, I tell people about it. And in right circumstances, I try to share my faith. I do that when I write a book or speak on television.

Harold Kushner: How do I deal with people whose religious commitments are on a collision course with my religious commitments? I disagree with them, but I respect them. We Jews are not intent on ringing doorbells and looking for converts. The Jewish mission is not to help the world become Jewish, but to bring the world to God. We want to bring the world to God by modeling rather than by pressuring or nagging.

Going back to our history at Sinai, God seems to say to us that most people can learn how to live not from books, but from living models. Therefore we Jewish people want to be an example. God gives us the book to read, to digest, and to live by in order that we can model God's love.

I try to entice people into the righteousness of my perspective not by arguing or quoting scripture continuously, but simply by living the kind of life that moves people to say, "I would like to have the serenity and focused purpose and spur to activism that Harold Kushner has." People don't have to become Jewish to attain this, or to agree with me on every-

I'm not afaid of heretics, I'm not afraid of freethinkers, I'm not afraid of people who want to challenge the tradition.

John Spong

thing, but essentially to affirm the kind of moral direction I've rooted my life in. This type of witnessing is what I'm trying to do by modeling. I don't do it by saying, "I think you're wrong, and let me tell you why." I do it by saying, "This is where I'm coming from and where it leads me and why I find it satisfying."

John Spong: I see the Christian life as the rolling of a river or stream. I see myself being carried along somewhat on the wave of the tradition, but also exploring. A river does some interesting things. Sometimes it bends and goes in a different direction, just like religion and the history of faith do at times. Sometimes a new path is cut by a small part of the river while a major portion will go on. If that new path turns out to be a dead end, then ultimately it hits the dead end and comes back to the major stream. But there are times when the main path turns out to be the dead end, and it was only the little tributary that offered continuation of the flow and became the major path.

This is an example of what happens with people and religion, too. That's why I'm not afraid of heretics, I'm not afraid of freethinkers, I'm not afraid of people who want to challenge the tradition. I want people to know the tradition; you can't challenge what you don't know. I want us to know the tradition and take it seriously, but also to be willing to move away from it in wonderful new directions.

HOW DO WE RIGHT THE WRONG?

Harold Kushner: Religion has to be involved with social issues. We saw what religion could do in the dimly remembered days of the 1960s, when it was one of the main motivating forces for the civil rights movement, and to some degree for the anti-war effort.

Religion gives people a vision of what the world would look like if it were truly God's world. It gives people a vision of how we might be able to get along together. It calls us to account and asks us why the world isn't like that.

I don't know to what extent churches should put their priority on social action. I've asked myself why I haven't done more. I used to be very active in the civil rights movement in the sixties. What's happened? Have I grown older? Has the world gotten more complicated? I used to think it was so simple. You go out and carry a picket sign and quote Isaiah and people listen to you and become good people.

We've found out it's a lot more complicated than that. We discovered the law of unintended consequences. All sorts of good things we thought we were doing turned out to bring complications in their wake.

I have found my calling more in the individual, pastoral dimension than in the community-action dimension. Yet at the same time, I have done something. My synagogue has done something. Other synagogues and churches have held aloft the banner of what the world should be like. We have had to learn that the world is a lot more complicated and that religious slogans won't do it. Redemption comes as one tiny little grain of sand at a time.

Some churches and synagogues have been discouraged by this lesson. They thought they could bring the Messiah within six months and with a limited budget. When they found out they could barely make a dent in the problem, they gave up.

We are working. The churches that provide refuge for one person fleeing an oppressive government in Central America, the churches that build low-income housing in an affluent suburb for twelve or fifteen impoverished families, the churches that collect food and clothing for the homeless, they're not bringing redemption single-handedly. But they're making the world one-tenth of one degree warmer, and that's a great achievement.

I used to think it was so simple. You go out and carry a picket sign and quote Isaiah and people listen to you and become good people.

Harold Kushner

James Forbes: The church is a strange body these days. Some churches are attempting to make real the gospel so that it addresses the problem of resource distribution, of intergroup relationships, of peace, and those types of issues.

But I'm disturbed about the church when it is only a place that helps you recover from the threat of life to your own sense of well-being. It is a comfort station, and thank God for comfort stations. We need them at times. My problem is that too many churches have become primarily comfort stations. They comfort their homogeneous population and reassure them that "All is going to be well." They tell people that God will bless them because they do the "right" things. They get in their cozy little comfort station and it takes the Spirit and God and everyone else to get them outside of that.

The church today appears to me to be much more interested in reassuring people that "God is with us" than it is in equipping people to go forth as God's agent, to let people outside the precincts of the privileged know that God has special concerns for them.

Ada Maria Isasi-Diaz: The ongoing split between a few very wealthy persons and the majority of the poor is overwhelming us. I work for an organization called Church Women United, which soon will be celebrating its fiftieth anniversary. It has won great respect in the community. The women work very hard and engage in all kinds of soup kitchens and similar projects. But it seems that no matter how hard these people work, they can't even meet the needs they used to be able to meet. The needs are so astronomical that we can't claim success for the "band-aid" kind of solutions that we are used to.

We have to turn things around. I helped put out a booklet entitled *Perfect Charity Brings Forth Justice.* We have to work so more and more people in our communities understand the economics of poverty. We just can't continue to work within a system where there are a few very rich while a vast majority are poor. The poorest are women and children, and that's of particular interest to me. Our society needs to change radically.

Will Campbell: The institutional church stands precisely where the rich young ruler stood. The church is rich. The institutional church is very, very rich. It's good. I don't accuse it of being a "bad" outfit. But Jesus said, "Never mind that. Get rid of it and then come back and we'll talk about discipleship afterwards."

Robert McAfee Brown: The institutional Catholic Church in Central America has sided with the rich for centuries. It played into the concerns of the rich and blessed those efforts. In recent times, this has begun to change and there have been preferential options for the poor among many in the church.

Now the rich come along and say, "That's dirty pool. You're supposed to be for everybody. How come you're taking sides all of a sudden?"

The only answer the church can give is that they're not taking sides; rather, they're changing sides. "You never objected when we unequivocally supported your great land estates. Now we see that that's contrary to the gospel. We've got to be for the poor initially, not just to 'destroy' you, but so all people can have a share of God's creation and can see indeed that God loves all people."

God has to love the rich because some stark demands are placed on them; that's the side of love that folks like us don't want to hear.

We don't say, "Come into the body of Christ. Come into my church. Sit next to me." If we've failed at this point, we've failed at it all.

Delores Williams

Delores Williams: The church has to look at the way it is involved in exploitation through what it professes to believe and the way it supports what it does, and what it does *not* support. The church knows who the poor and needy are. We have poor, hungry people walking the streets. But we don't—and I include my church and myself too—we don't invite those people into the body of Christ, even though we might have programs to help the needy.

We don't say, "Come into the body of Christ. Come into my church. Sit next to me." If we've failed at this point, we've failed at it all.

Virginia Mollenkott: It's the church's book that tells us about loving our neighbor as ourself. The church's role—at its best, not at its worst—is to hold up a vision and provide rituals, the mythological substructuring that we all need. I've seen people burn out in various social activist movements because they had no myth. The surge of the Spirit is very important when you're working for human justice. The church can provide the enactment in the Eucharist, for instance, of human oneness.

Daniel Berrigan: I have a very deep sense of what the church can offer, and also what the church is offering. Americans would have invaded Nicaragua several years ago if it hadn't been for the American church, and perhaps more specifically, for the American Catholic Church. This was the only restraining factor on an absolutely mad march toward wiping those people out. The government couldn't quite get away with it and they haven't done it, as of now, because of the church. That's marvelous and very important.

Not much is being said outside the church about the nuclear question, at least not much that makes sense to me. The clarity of the Methodist bishops is absolutely admirable. "Ah, no deterrents…Get rid of them." It's very simple. No nuclear weapons in any human hands.

Peter Berger: I'm at odds with the common view in mainline Protestant and Catholic churches in the West, which believes that the church ought constantly to take positions and take sides in every conceivable and social conflict. To do that is a terrible mistake. The church is typically incompetent to make intelligent contributions to discussions in areas that social scientists know something about. What church bodies have said has been either wrong or very trivial and therefore unhelpful.

Most of the time the church's role is useful and deals with what religious experience is all about. The church as an institution witnesses to the fact that ordinary human life, including social issues, is not the last word on human existence. There is something beyond this. Any particular social justice issue is relatively unimportant. What finally matters is what God does with the world and with human beings in eternity.

Now that's what the church testifies to, what its message is all about. It's not about social issues. But if you believe that message, the social issues look different. They're put in a much larger context. That's an enormous contribution of the church.

The church as an institution witnesses to the fact that ordinary human life, including social issues, is not the last word on human existence.

Peter Berger

Robert Raines: In a democracy we say we cannot leave it to the military experts to decide things about war and peace. The people have to be involved. The church doesn't have any special information, but it has a special value system. It has a special concern. There's something "subversive" about a faithful Jewish synagogue or Christian congregation, subversive in the sense of always being subversive of any status quo regarding what is not yet fair, just, equitable, passionate in that place. Inevitably, if the church is being faithful, it will always be jabbing, nudging, asking questions until the end of time.

Martin Marty: The Christian community is probably better off when it's fifty percent on each side of various issues, as long as each side is listening and challenging the other. So I'm not claiming special knowledge, wisdom, or skill for the church. I am claiming a special impulse. We go into it even if we are going to lose in the sense that the world counts "losing."

For example, a county road commissioner has a lot of work and not too much pay. The job is not glamorous, but if the potholes are gone, our lives are saved because someone didn't have to swerve (often we didn't even know the potholes in the road). It's politics.

I see politics as a rather modest human art that prevents things from happening. Without politics, we'd be in the jungle, we'd be chaotic, there would be totalitarianism. Politics is a means by which all of the elements that make up society—factions, sex, interest groups, caucuses, movements, churches, etc.—get something out of the order because they put into it. If you're apathetic and politics overwhelms you, I don't feel sorry for you. If you've put energy into organizing sets of people who stand for good things and you raise some funds and twist some arms and use good speeches and endure, you should get something back out of it. It's a marvelous instrument for civil peace and responsibility.

Will Campbell: Politics is the enemy. Always. Power does corrupt. I've always been suspicious of social movements even though I've been involved in a few all of my adult life. But again, I've never trusted any of them. Because it's the assumption that "If we take this thing over, we're

I'm not claiming special knowledge, wisdom, or skill for the church. I am claiming a special impulse. We go into it even if we are going to lose in the sense that the world counts "losing."

Martin Marty

going to do it better." Throughout history we've never done it better. We've become like the things we've detested.

When I was helping deserters and dodgers get to Canada during the Vietnam war, was that political? I was saying to Caesar "The State can do anything it wants to do by definition of the word. But I'm not going to help you. I'm not going to assist you in this carnage. And if these young people feel that they cannot help you, then I'm going to assist them."

One side of the coin can call that a political action. To me it was a matter of Christian discipleship to say no to Caesar. The same thing is true in the civil rights movement.

It's off target to say, "Because I have this burning desire for justice, I'm going to become president of the United States and get you guys straightened out," which many politicians do.

Robert McAfee Brown: We have to be deeply involved. One of the great heresies of our time is to say that religion and politics don't mix. From the Exodus story and on, they're mixing all over the place. Jeremiah comes along and says, in effect, "To know God is to do justice." If you're not trying to do justice, you don't know God. You're, in effect, an atheist. The connection is inseparable. Jesus says, "If you're not feeding the hungry and clothing the naked and visiting the sick...all these so-called social justice issues...you're rejecting me. If you're helping those people, you're responding to me."

The people who have to defend their stand are those who are not involved, not those who are involved.

Rosemary Radford Ruether: We have a delusional notion that there's some kind of religion that's unpolitical and then, if people get involved in justice, that's political. But in fact what we have to begin with is a religion that is on the side of the unjust status quo, that's political on the side of injustice, that masks itself as being spiritual and unpolitical. But it's not unpolitical at all. It's never been that way. It's called "royal theology" and sacralizes systems of unjust power. It's still a dominant form of religion throughout history.

What prophetic religion is about is criticizing...and putting the power of religious faith on the side of change.

Rosemary Radford Ruether

What prophetic religion is about is criticizing that and putting the power of religious faith on the side of change.

Jim Wallis: Should faith have anything to do with life? When we raise these polarizations, I have to laugh. They're "white" people's church questions. For the church of the poor and black churches, that's not a question. The idea that you could care about someone's prayer life and not care whether they have any food to eat or have a job, or if unspeakable violence is being committed against someone, would never enter the mind of someone who's reading the Bible from any normal perspective. It only enters your mind if you're comfortable and insulated and removed from these problems; then the church getting involved in "these problems" has nothing to do with your life. When you ask these questions, you have to look at where you're sitting and asking them from.

The God of the Bible is a deliverer of the poor and has a special love for the disenfranchised, the marginalized, those who are the bottom of everyone else's priority list. If that isn't clear from the Bible, then I would say nothing is clear from the Bible. That is the message in the Bible from start to finish.

One time, while I was in seminary, my friends and I decided to do an experiment. We got an old Bible and a pair of scissors and we cut out of the Bible, Old Testament and New Testament, every single reference to the poor, every time the poor were named: "God is on the side of the poor." "The gospel is good news for the poor." We cut all those verses out. When we were done we had a Bible that was literally in shreds. It would not stay together. I used to go out and preach with that Bible and hold it up high in front of American congregations and say, " Brothers and sisters, this is the American Bible, full of holes."

The Bible is clear. The poor of the world, who are the growing church all over the world, understand this. For them it is a tremendous source of hope and comfort and power that God is with them in their struggle, helping them survive—for life, for justice, and for a decent future for their family. These things are very clear.

WHAT GIVES YOU FAITH?

Martin Marty: I came into my faith gradually. I was nurtured in a Christian home where all those meanings were available, but every serious adult says "That's their faith, not mine. They've tried to impart it to me."

Faith has to be appropriated and become your own. For me it didn't come in a blinding flash. It didn't come as a datable moment when I could say I had been "born again." It comes through "billions of particulars," the highs and lows of adolescence, the early years of marriage, child rearing, death and remarriage, passages of life, and moments of special intensity when you ask, "Did the things I thought to be true end up being worth certifying for the future?" My faith developed through billions of particulars, through wrestling and acceptance of the gift of grace. Those are the places where I can look back and see the "activity of God."

I can't point to high drama. I live a 51 percent to 49 percent life emotionally. I have what Dag Hammarskjöld called a Yes to life with a capital Y. It's saying, "That person is a friend and not an enemy." "This day is a gift instead of a burden."

Rosemary Radford Ruether: I grew up as a Roman Catholic and had very good role models, particularly in my mother who had a mature faith. She had a sense of truthfulness and integrity. I was encouraged to ask critical questions in high school and college like "What does all this mean?" My mother thought it was excellent for me to be asking those types of questions. That is the way you grow and become an authentic person. So I gradually worked out what I thought was an authentic relationship to God and how that related to the historical tradition.

A lot of my faith developed through historical study, going back and trying to understand the context in which early Christianity arose and how it was related to the Jewish tradition, and working out a relationship to that tradition that didn't have to falsify some part of reality, didn't have to pretend things had happened historically that didn't happen, etc. I learned to make some kind of integral connection between faith and knowledge.

Madeleine L'Engle: I was a cradle Episcopalian born to cradle Episcopalians whose parents had been cradle Episcopalians. But my father had been gassed in the First World War. It took him until I was almost eighteen to finish coughing his lungs out. He worked best in the afternoons and evenings. So my parents slept late, and on Sunday there was no one to take me to Sunday school. I feel very blessed about this. I've met so many people who've had to spend their grown-up life unlearning all of the stuff they learned in Sunday school about a forensic, punitive God.

I never got that. I started out with a God of love. My parents thought I might enjoy the Bible because it had good stories in it. Nobody told me it was a moral book. It isn't. It's a wonderful storybook about unqualified people.

That was a very good start. I didn't have a lot of dogma to unlearn. Yesterday's heresy becomes tomorrow's dogma. I went right at it from the point of view of story. God is the great storyteller.

Virginia Mollenkott: There were many, many years when I had to admit I didn't know if there was a God or if there was a God who loved me. The change came about when my masculine image of God was shattered and when I "floated" around, not understanding but working with the Bible and trying to understand its multiplicity of images.

Speaking to people also helped me. Every time you tell an audience or someone in particular that God loves them, you believe it a little more about yourself.

Dan Wakefield: There's a wonderful phrase in the Bible about the prodigal son after he goes off and lives tumultuously and wastefully. The line says, "And then he came to himself." I was tremendously moved by that line. I still am, because returning to faith felt like that to me. It wasn't something strange or bizarre or coming into some new experience. It was like coming home in the deepest kind of way. You come not to something foreign or some new discovery or special knowledge, but you come to yourself.

I was very relieved when a minister told us that the word for conversion, both in Greek and Hebrew, meant "turning." That seemed to describe my process, rather than a zap of lightning out of the sky—and then sud-

The change came about when my masculine image of God was shattered and when I "floated" around, not understanding but working with the Bible and trying to understand its multiplicity of images.

Virginia Mollenkott

Through a long personal struggle I realized one day that my image of God is like a middle-aged Korean woman looking like my mother—warm, affirming, available.

Hyung Kyung Chung

denly I understood. It was a slow turning. *Returning* seemed a way of describing that process. It still goes on.

Hyung Kyung Chung: Being a Christian in my culture, which is a pagan culture, means denying the culture. Christianity came to my culture and is very imperialistic and colonialistic. It's almost schizophrenic; your heart and body are Korean and your head is European.

As a theological student I always thought that God was a spirit and not an image. But I had an image of God as a Caucasian man with blue eyes, long hair, with a big nose and a white robe. My intellectual side said, "God has no image. God is spirit." But all my upbringing as a Christian in Korea in a Korean church that was founded by Western missionaries, all my Sunday school education, was based on this picture of God who looks like

Moses in the movie *The Ten Commandments*.

Through a long personal struggle I realized one day that my image of God is like a middle-aged Korean woman looking like my mother—very warm, affirming, available, strong, and "down to earth." When I pray, this image comes to me. This is my image of God now. It's very liberating because before, when I prayed to God who was white, who was old, who was a man, it was difficult for me to feel connected with him.

Daniel Berrigan: I don't know if there is any easy way, but mine was not easy. It's sort of "following your nose." You hit up against a lot of walls and your nose gets bruised. I got certain leads from my own family, from friends, from scripture study, from the real Jesuit tradition (which is not necessarily being verified in America any more than the Christian tradition is verified ordinarily).

I don't want to claim that I follow those leads impeccably or even in a way I can be proud of. But I know I have the leads. I guess the word for that is *grace*.

Desmond Tutu: When I was twelve years old I had tuberculosis. At one time I was quite sick, hemorrhaging, and I was taken to a TB hospital. The other patients used to tell one another that anyone who was as sick as I was, hemorrhaging so much, was going to die. On this particular occasion I just said, "Well, if I'm going to die, that's okay." I hope this doesn't sound heroic because it wasn't heroic. It wasn't anything I said feeling spectacular and courageous or even religious. I just said, "Well, if it happens, it happens." I said, "I'm committing myself to you, God," and an extraordinary calm descended over me.

Roy Sano: Because we were Japanese in the United States during World War II, the federal agents were sent to pick up my father and other leaders of the community so that they wouldn't foment any resistance or demonstrations. They were hauled off to Bismarck, North Dakota, ostensibly to see if there were any espionage agents or saboteurs among them. (They didn't find any.)

As a teenager I was saying, "I want to bank my life on islands of acceptance like this community of faith."

Roy Sano

The rest of us went to the camps without dad, and then finally he was released after six months. Some of our Japanese neighbors in the camp used to hold prayer meetings in our part of the barracks. Probably hearing those songs, the hymns of the faith, and seeing people with composure despite the breakdown of our lives, these kinds of conscious influences shaped my faith—that people could live with dignity in the face of abuse.

During the "Death of God" debate in the sixties, I kept thinking, "I should really try to doubt God."

Walter Wink

Although theologically it raises some strange questions, I was rebaptized at that time. We went out to the Colorado River and I was immersed. Baptism is death and resurrection and means getting rid of certain things, being freed up. But United Methodists generally believe in dabbling, not in immersion. When they immersed me, it was a desperate attempt on my parents' part to ask God to get us out of that situation. They were hoping for a new beginning.

The faith of my family, which I might call a "hand-me-down" faith, was nevertheless a very important formative factor.

When I was a teenager in Pennyslvania, I came under the influence of a wonderful pastor who at a camp meeting invited me to come forward and accept Jesus as my Lord and Savior. When I went forward at that camp meeting, an overwhelming sense of relief overtook me as I knelt at the altar. I started to cry uncontrollably. I felt embarrassed and left as soon as I could. When I got off the bus, I just wanted to run the half mile home.

Reflecting on that experience, I realize that as a teenager I was saying, "I want to bank my life on islands of acceptance like this community of faith." Later I came to realize that other factors were involved. But that was the beginning, when I was given the opportunity to make a public response to all the gestures that contradict hostility and hatred.

Walter Wink: When I was nineteen years old, I had a very profound mystical experience. It was so overwhelmingly real that God has seemed more real than reality as a result. In fact, during the sixties and the "Death of God" debate, I kept thinking, "I should really try to doubt God." I tried several times but I couldn't rouse myself toward even a mild skepticism, because I knew that this reality was so powerful. It's just never left me.

I've left God, I've wandered, I've been asleep, I've been unresponsive, but I've never felt that God has left me. I've never felt God's desertion. I'm very lucky in that respect. I'm also very grateful.

Dan Wakefield: Do I share my faith? There's a wonderful phrase of William Buckley's, who said in an interview with Malcolm Muggeridge, "I don't know how it is in England, but in New York, if you mention God more than once at a dinner party, you're not invited back." That could happen to me. I could not be invited back.

Today I certainly do speak openly about my faith. I've written a whole book about it, so I can't avoid it. I find that people for the most part, even friends who don't think of themselves as religious, are respectful and say things like, "I once had an inkling of that" or "I once had that." It's wrong of us to try to hide our convictions.

Roy Sano: I tend to share my faith when it's the expected thing to do. I'm learning a new job in the last few years since coming into the episcopacy. I've let my life become too "churchianified." I need to interact more with the world, share my faith more with the world, and talk to people in different areas of life.

Daniel Berrigan: One doesn't concoct a religious vocabulary in order to share one's faith. A lot of it is nonverbal anyway. It's body language. It's style. It's aura. When I sit with a dying person, as I'm going to be doing later today, he knows that I'm there for him. He's not explicitly a religious person who summons a lot of religious language himself. What he's doing with his life is dying well, which is a religious activity of the highest order. What I'm trying to do as a religious person is to be with him in that awesome passage he's making. I'm sharing my faith with him and he with me.

Rosemary Radford Ruether: Faith is a way of living justly and lovingly. It's a total life style. That essentially is the way I try to perform everything I do. If I'm engaged in teaching, I'm trying to give the most authentic account of what this truth is about and really encourage students to

What he's doing with his life is dying well, which is a religious activity of the highest order. What I'm trying to do as a religious person is to be with him in that awesome passage that he's making.

Daniel Berrigan

become self-seekers for truth, to go beyond reading a book to get a grade. I want students to become autonomous truth-seekers. We need to connect this struggle for truth with the struggle for justice and make connections between theory and practice.

Virginia Mollenkott: I love to watch students come alive. One of the courses I teach is freshman English, and that's a place where you can empower people. They often come to you beaten down. All anyone had done was tell them how bad they were in English. You try to encourage them to write about who they are, to talk about who they are, and you show some interest in them. You show them that they have something interesting in their lives. They're people.

Before I pass back their first graded paper, I give them a little speech: "This grade is not for you. This grade is for a piece of work you turned in."

Then I ask them if they want to know what I think of them, and usually they want to. So I continue, "I think you're made in the image of God and of inestimable worth. There's no way anything I could put in my grade book could ever begin to estimate you."

I learned to do this after I read Flannery O'Connor's story about the boy who went up in the attic and drew a circle with a big "F" in the middle because he hadn't been doing well in school, and hanged himself over the "F." He didn't distinguish between the grade he was getting and who he was.

For me, the meaning of life is to share with people the wonderful news that we are the daughters and sons of God.

WHAT HAPPENS AFTER DEATH?

Desmond Tutu: You couldn't not think about death when you live in South Africa and receive death threats frequently. Like many others, I've tended to push it to the back of my mind and forget that "We all suffer from a terminal disease." We are all going to die. We pretend that this is not one of the most fundamental things about us.

Ada Maria Isasi-Diaz: I wholeheartedly believe that death is not the end. It is incongruous with my belief about God. I don't see relationships as something you can put an end to. Once a relationship is established, it has to keep evolving. If God is love and a relationship with the divine is about love, then I need to believe that there's something beyond death that is going to continue the sort of relationship with God and each other that I have worked toward in this life.

Harold Kushner: Death is the end of the body. At death my physical properties—my respiration, my circulation, my digestion—stop. I'm buried. Over the course of years the physical "me" dissolves and returns to the earth.

But I can't stop there, because I insist that the real "me" is not my body. I can change my body. I can lose weight, I can gain weight, cut my hair, color my hair, look different, age, wrinkle, but I'm still the same me. The real me is my values, my ideas, my commitments, my memory, my sense of humor—what I would label under the old religious word "soul."

I have to believe that because a soul is not a physical thing, a soul doesn't die. But my body does. That's as much as I can understand.

What I cannot begin to comprehend is what happens to a soul when it doesn't have a body. My mind is three-dimensional and can only think in three-dimensional physical terms. What does it mean for a soul to exist when it's not incarnated in a body? That's like asking, "Where does an idea go when I forget it?" or "Where was the idea before I thought of it?" or "What happens to jokes that people don't tell any more? Is there a storehouse for them?"

Where are non-physical things when they're not embodied? I don't know. At some level I have to believe that my soul will continue after I die. Will it know that it used to be me? Will it be capable of feeling joy without optic nerves, without a brain, without a glandular/endocrine sys-

*W*e are all going to die. We pretend that this is not one of the most fundamental things about us.

Desmond Tutu

tem? Will it be able to recognize other disembodied souls?

Having said that my body disappears after death and my soul survives, I also have to say something else. I believe that just as in the world of physical properties there's a law of conservation of matter (that is, my body doesn't disappear, it decays and becomes part of the earth, etc.), in the world of good and evil, there's a law of conservation of spiritual energy. That is, no good deed is ever wasted. No selfish, wicked deed is ever totally gotten away with. For me, hell is not a place where they stick you with pitchforks. Hell is realizing that if I was sarcastic to my daughter when she was a little girl, she will be sarcastic to my grandchildren. If I told a lie five years ago, it will end up causing two strangers to end up mistrusting each other five years from now.

For me, conversely, heaven is not blue skies and soft music and harps. Heaven is knowing that if I tried to do something right and was not able to, somebody will have been moved by that example and will do something right years from now because they were inspired by me. There is a law of conserving the good deeds that I do; they're not totally wasted.

As a physician you whisper in someone's ear, "We love you. Your love will stay with us. It's okay to go." And people go.

Bernie Siegel

Elisabeth Schüssler Fiorenza: I think about people who have died in terms of their life having made a difference and of being alive in our memories. People have really died if there's no person, no group, or no tradition around that still loves them. People die only when they die in our love and in our memory. Therefore, people can die and still be very present and effective in our lives.

Bernie Siegel: If you want to be immortal, love someone. Your love stays. You live on in everyone and everything. You can't be immortal physically, but in another sense we can live on in some other form. I don't remember dying and doing this before, so I don't have obvious evidence.

As a physician you whisper in someone's ear, "We love you. Your love will stay with us. It's okay to go." And people go.

James Carroll: A friend of mine said, "Life is just an escalator. We're all going up. Some people are older and some are younger, but we're all going up."

I thought that was an interesting image so I asked him, "What's at the top?"

"There's nothing at the top; we just fall off," he said.

Being at the top is the moment of feeling "Why have you forsaken me?" I don't say that to be glib about the afterlife. I don't assume anything about heaven. I think my friend is right: we fall off. But in that falling we learn the meaning of "Into your hands in faith I allow myself to fall," not clinging, not making of life itself a kind of false God. I don't want to die, and I don't want my parents to die or my children or my wife. But they're going to die and I'm going to die. We seem incapable of directly contemplating death; that, of course, is the ultimate denial. Do you remember the great dream we have of falling? We always wake up before we hit the bottom because we can't sustain a real image of death not even in our dreams. We all live—and apparently sleep—assuming our immortality.

Daniel Berrigan: We're not promised immortality. We're promised resurrection. Those are very different matters. The first I take to be a poisoned culture word which is close to the imperial adventure. Americans want desperately to be immortal which, in Christian terms, means they don't want to die. The result of that mad quest for immortality is that you have to kill others.

Roy Sano: I'm very uncomfortable in this society because we want to move too quickly to resurrection or resolution of problems. One of the central symbols of Protestant Christianity is a levitating, shining cross. I think this is a heresy. It's the kind of heresy the early church had when a person of Christ believed that Jesus was so divine he couldn't be touching the ground. Our emphasis on resurrection has become heretical because it cannot incorporate death as integral to that story along with the resurrection. That's why I keep telling people, "At least drape the cross with some dark tones of color."

When I see pastel colors in Lent, I feel this is a scandal, because they've not been able to take the deep and darker realities of life. They want to run from it. They turn to Christianity to wipe all of this out, which I find offensive to what I regard as a central part of our faith. It is *death and resurrection*.

Bernie Siegel: What I say to people is that "Visiting hours are over and the touch is gone." A little boy said he was afraid of the thunder and lightning. His father told him that God would take care of him, "not to worry." "Sometimes, I need God with skin on," the little boy responded.

Well, there's a loss of "the skin," the physical contact, the visiting. I wear a maple leaf and use that as a symbol because it's one of God's ways of telling us what life is about. You're born. You look like all the other leaves. You realize you're going to die. You get rid of the cover-up, the green. You show your true beauty and uniqueness. And when you get tired of hanging onto the tree of life, you let go and die. But when you've shown your beauty, you say, "I'm tired and I'm leaving now."

Death means there's a separation and loss. Tears are involved. Grief is involved. But it's not painful because you're tired and sore and you believe that "My next healing is leaving this body." If you haven't lived and nobody has loved you and you've been abused, it's hard to die.

Again, speaking as a physician, I know that most people die at 2:00 a.m. because they feel like failures, and when their families aren't there they sneak out of their body. (I see it in a very different context of hoping to get people to live so they can die at 3:00 p.m. or at sunrise.) One boy said he wanted to wait until sunset. And so at sunset, when it was beautiful and he was surrounded in love by his family, he died. He left his family with a gift.

Harvey Cox: I'm not one of those people who's able to say, "Ah, death is a part of life and we all die sometime." Realistically and honestly, I have to say it's terrible. The thought of being deprived of the companionship of my family, my children, the joys of human life, carries with it a horror for me which I cannot dilute with some kind of religious diminishing of this fact. I don't think this is contradictory in any way to religious faith. Jesus did not want to die. He went into the garden and asked if there was any way he could get out of it. He even asked God, "Please get me out of it."

Walter Wink: Nothing is lost. God gathers up everything into her   breast. A person being tortured, who dies without witnesses, is gathered up into

Nothing is lost. God gathers up everything into her breast. A person being tortured, who dies without witnesses, is gathered up into God, and that death is not in vain.

Walter Wink

God, and that death is not in vain. The weight of that death is another snowflake on the branch that will somehow make it snap. God is a guarantor that justice will somehow finally be done on earth as it is is heaven.

Desmond Tutu: There is a kind of suffering that needs a redressing that I don't think can happen this side of life. I'm not talking about "pie in the sky" when we die. Ultimately there will be a vindication of the goodness of God: when we enjoy the beatitude of being in the presence of God and recognize that life was not all nonsense, that there was meaning. My Africanness leads me to believe that my dead mother still cares for me. Also, my dead father has an interest in me and is concerned. Maybe I'm naive about this, but I'd rather be naive than cynical.

Hyung Kyung Chung: We Koreans believe that when our father and mother and grandfather and grandmother die, if they lived a good life, they can let go of this world and go to paradise. They come back and visit us as if on vacation on our ancestor worship day, or their birthdays or their funeral days. So we have feasts together and talk to them. We open all the windows at midnight because we believe their spirit comes through the windows. I feel a real connection with Central Americans in Nicaragua and El Salvador when their comrades die in revolutionary struggle. In their worship services they call the individuals who died by name and really believe they are present with them. I can accept that kind of faith. It's very much connected to my own culture, my own tradition. At the same time, the Christian tradition is also true.

Carmen Guerrero: My mother and father both died within a six-month span of time when I was in seminary. It was a very difficult time for me, partly because I had just begun to discover who my father was, not physically, but emotionally. I had just met him, and then a year later he died of cancer. Six months later my mother was gone. It was the first time in my life that anybody who was close to me had died. The "communion of saints" took on a totally different meaning for me. It was no longer just words.

I communicate more with them now, but not in the sense of calling their spirit or hearing voices. They're very real, sometimes much more real than when they were alive.

James Forbes: Occasionally I get the impression that mom has some sense of what is going on. I have no theology for that statement. But it is at least my linkage with her beyond the grave. I can say, "Hey mom, how am I doing?" Do I expect an answer? No. Do I expect a visitation in the night? No. But I have some sense of our spirits as being connected. The church talks about it as the "communion of saints." I don't understand it. But I get the feeling that there is a connection for which my earthly language is inadequate. My heart has a sense that the breakage between the moment of death and life has not been thorough and that tubes of connection exist even now.

Bernie Siegel: I've dealt with thousands of people who are dead, and I feel like they're around my shoulders. They're part of my prayers and meditations. I talk to a lot of people regularly who have died. They're always around. They're special people who have taught me a lot. I have this cluster of people that I talk to every morning.

Now if you don't mind being considered crazy you can talk about these things. Go to a meeting where all the parents have had a child die...murder, cancer, an accident...horrendous stories. Introduce yourself and then talk. Everyone is in a safe place. Those parents will tell you stories about how their children have come back, saved their lives, appeared in the bedroom, kept them out of an auto accident...incredible events that have happened. If those parents walk out of that room, no one else will hear their stories. They know they're safe in that room because everyone has experienced similar stories and it's okay to share them. When you're in secret and safe, you hear a lot of things about which you'd publicly say, "That's crazy." "How can that happen?" People who have had these experiences will say, "Well, okay, I'm not going to talk about it."

Madeleine L'Engle: It's not the nature of love to create and then annihilate. If I believe God is love, then I have to believe that what has been made is

I get the feeling that there is a connection for which my earthly language is inadequate. My heart has a sense that the breakage between the moment of death and life has not been thorough.

James Forbes

going to go on being made. Have you seen that button that says "P B P G I N F W M Y"? The initials mean "please be patient, God is not finished with me yet." I have a lot more I want to learn. I'm nowhere nearly finished. I don't think I'm going to die without any chance of learning it all.

I took my granddaughter Charlotte down to North Florida where my mother's family settled in the late fifties. I wanted her to experience some of her North Florida roots. We went out to Fleming's Island (Fleming is a family name). There's a wonderful little Gothic church there which seats about a hundred people. To the back and to the sides is a beautiful old cemetery shaded with live oak trees. It's a very peaceful place. I've been there many times. This time it really hit me that those people who were put into those graves believed that their actual bodies, their bones, their skin, their blood and veins, were going to rise up at the last trumpet. Christians at the time could not be cremated because they believed God was not powerful enough to do anything with ashes. We don't believe that anymore. But the church has not gone any further in saying what it does believe.

When my husband was dying, the church was wonderful. When he died, they had nothing to say. The old platitudes don't work.

John Spong: I'm convinced that there is some survival of human consciousness past biological death. I affirm this statement on a lot of different levels. Most of the traditional patterns I've long ago rejected. I'm not interested in any of the traditional images of heaven. I don't care for milk or honey. I'm not interested in a place of reward or golden lampstands. I don't really like "righteous" people; they're the most unloving people I've ever confronted. Nor do I think individualistically. I don't believe you or I are responsible completely for any of the actions of our lives. If I'm not able to love, it's because I've never been loved. If I've been raised in abject poverty, I'm going to have a different value system than that of the majority. If I've been a victim of racial oppression, I'm going to have a certain amount of anger that was given to me.

We must take seriously the fact that we are deeply interdependent, both sociologically and psychologically. That's a frontier the scientific

When my husband was dying, the church was wonderful. When he died, they had nothing to say. The old platitudes don't work.

Madeleine L'Engle

world will open up in the next one hundred years and recognize that human life is incredibly interrelated. There really is no such thing as an individual. That's a myth out of our ignorance. That affects dramatically the religious concepts of life after death which in Christianity are based on a radical understanding of individualism: good deeds, bad deeds, scales, reward or punishment. I don't know how one does a good deed without recognizing all of the forces that helped make it possible for one to even think that way. Ultimately I suppose I am a universalist. I really believe that life after death is something that is open to every person. The thing that makes life after death real for me is the relationship we have with the God who is beyond the limits of our humanity.

Dayton Edmonds: These words come to me which are a birth song and a death song:

The Circle Again: Birth and Death

Do not stand at my grave and weep.
I am not there; I do not sleep.
I am a thousand winds that blow;
I am the diamond glimpse on snow;
I am the gentle autumn rain;
I am the sunripe golden grain.
And when you wake in the morning, hush.
I am the swift uplifting rush
of circling birds and circling flight;
I am the soft starlight at night.
Do not stand at my grave and weep.
I am not there; I do not sleep.

Peter Berger

The Rev. Daniel Berrigan

Peter Berger, a Lutheran sociologist, has directed the Institute for the Study of Economic Culture at Boston University since 1985. Widely respected as a sociologist of religion, he is the author of many books, including *The Sacred Canopy: Elements of a Sociological Theory of Religion, Religion in a Revolutionary Society, The Precarious Vision, Speaking to the Third World: Essays on Democracy* (coauthored with Michael Novak), and *To Empower People: The Role of Mediating Structures in Public Policy* (coauthored with Richard John Neuhaus).

The Rev. Daniel Berrigan is best known for his antiwar activities of the 1960s. His concern for social justice has made him a role model for those pursuing justice through nonviolent methods. He presently writes poetry and nonfiction, and ministers to AIDS patients in New York City. He has written fifteen books, including *Beside the Sea of Glass: The Song of the Lamb, Prison Poems, To Dwell in Peace, The Words Our Saviour Gave Us*, and *Portraits: O Those I Love*.

Robert McAfee Brown

Will Campbell

Robert McAfee Brown, teacher and author, is Emeritus Professor of Theology and Ethics at Pacific School of Religion in Berkeley, California. He has also taught at Amherst College, Union Theological Seminary (New York), Macalester College, Stanford University, and Pacific School of Religion. An active participant in justice efforts, Dr. Brown is recognized as the foremost interpreter in the United States of liberation theology. Among his more than twenty books are *The Spirit of Protestantism, The Ecumenical Revolution, Theology in a New Key, Making Peace in the Global Village,* and *Unexpected News: Reading the Bible with Third World Eyes.*

Besides farming forty acres in Mt. Juliet, Tennesee, where he grows corn, beans, tomatoes, watermelon, lima beans, and okra, Will Campbell writes books and country music (he once worked as the cook for Waylan Jennings). His books include *Race and the Renewal of the Church, Up to Our Steeples in Politics* (with James Holloway), *Brother to a Dragonfly, The Glad River, God on Earth,* and *Forty Acres and a Goat.* In the course of his career he has worked for the Committee of Southern Churchmen, served as chaplain at the University of Mississippi where he was involved in the civil rights movement, and headed the Southern Office of Racial and Cultural Relations of the National Council of Churches.

James Carroll

After ordination to the Roman Catholic priesthood in 1969, James Carroll served as chaplain at Boston University until 1974, leaving the priesthood in 1975. He was a regular columnist for *The National Catholic Reporter* from 1973 through 1976 and winner of the "Best Column Award" of the Catholic Press Association in 1976. He has been a full-time writer since 1975 and has written several books, plays, and a collection of poetry. His best-known books are *The Prince of Peace, Madonna Red, Fault Lines, The Winter of God, Family Trade,* and *Supply Heroes.*

Dr. Ignacio Castuera

Prior to his present appointment as senior pastor at First United Methodist Church in Hollywood, Dr. Ignacio Castuera served for five years as Los Angeles District Superintendent in the Pacific Southwest Conference of the United Methodist Church. He has also served churches in Mexico and Hawaii, and has taught theology as adjunct faculty at the School of Theology at Claremont.

Hyung Kyung Chung,

William Sloane Coffin, Jr.

Hyung Kyung Chung, a Presbyterian theologian, currently serves as Professor of Theology at Ewha Woman's University in Korea. She has been recognized as a leader in feminist theology and brings an Asian perspective to Christian thought.

William Sloane Coffin, Jr, was chaplain at Yale University for eighteen years, during which time he was named one of the original advisors to the newly established Peace Corps program. From 1977 through 1987 he served as senior minister of Riverside Church in New York City. On Christmas Eve, 1979, he was one of three U.S. clergy invited by the Iranian government to conduct Christmas services for the American hostages held in Iran. He began work as president of SANE/Freeze, a national organization that opposes nuclear testing and advocates international peace, in 1988. His books include *The Courage to Live* and *Living the Truth in a World of Illusions.*

Harvey G. Cox

Harvey G. Cox, a Baptist theologian, is Victor S. Thomas Professor of Divinity at Harvard Divinity School where he is best known as teacher of the course "Jesus and the Moral Life." His recent studies in Hinduism and Buddhism have established him as a leader in interfaith dialogues. Among his numerous books are *The Secular City, Religion in the Secular City, Many Mansions: A Christian's Encounter with Other Faiths,* and *The Silencing of Leonardo Boff: Liberation Theology and the Future of World Christianity.*

Dayton Edmonds

Born into a Native American tribe, Dayton Edmonds was thirteen when his father had a vision and became a Methodist minister. Today, Dayton Edmonds serves as a principal advocate for Native American rights. He is perhaps best known for his storytelling skills, which bring together Native American spirituality and Christian thought.

The Rev. Dr. James Forbes

The Rev. Dr. James Forbes is currently senior minister at New York's famed Riverside Church. He is known as one of the most forceful and inspirational preachers in the U.S. Before assuming his present post, Dr. Forbes was Professor of Preaching at Union Theological Seminary in New York.

Mary Gordon

Mary Gordon grew up in Queens, New York, where she attended Roman Catholic schools for twelve years before going to college. She is the author of four novels, *Final Payments, The Company of Women, Men and Angels,* and *The Other Side,* as well as a collection of short stories, *Temporary Shelters.* She lives in upstate New York with her husband and two children.

The Rev. Ms. Carmen Guerrero

The Rev. Ms. Carmen Guerrero, recently vicar of Santa Fe Church in San Antonio, Texas, is now the first full-time Hispanic missioner of the Episcopal Diocese of Los Angeles. While vicar in San Antonio, the mission was transformed from near abandonment to a thriving congregation, a development the Rev. Guerrero attributes to drawing upon the experiences of the Latin American base communities. Born in Corpus Christi, Texas, she attended the School of Theology at the University of the South, Sewanee, Tennessee, before being ordained to the priesthood in 1985 in Honduras. She worked for the Diocese of Honduras from 1984 to 1986 as coordinator of a theological education program that trained Hondurans for the priesthood.

Elisabeth Schüssler Fiorenza

Elisabeth Schüssler Fiorenza, a Roman Catholic theologian, is Professor of New Testament at Harvard Divinity School. She is the author of books on ministries of women in the church and on priesthood in the New Testament, as well as such biblical studies as *The Apocalypse* and *Invitation to Revelation.* She has written numerous articles on exegetical-theological issues and on feminist theology, and has served on various task forces and commissions on the problems of women in church and theology. In her major work, *In Memory of Her,* she reconstructs the origins of Christianity from a feminist perspective.

T. George Harris

Ada Maria Isasi-Diaz

Following his graduation from Yale University, T. George Harris studied social psychology at Oxford University's New College. In 1969 he became editor of *Psychology Today*. In 1982 Harris and his partner/publisher, Owen J. Lipstein, started *American Health Magazine*, which in 1985 won Columbia University's coveted journalism award for general excellence. The same award had been given to *Psychology Today* in 1973, making Harris the first editor ever to win it for two different magazines.

Born and educated in Cuba, Ada Maria Isasi-Diaz is presently program director for Church Women United. She is recognized as a theologian who is bridging Roman Catholic, feminist, and liberation theologies. She is one of the contributors to *God's Fierce Whimsey,* a collective theology written by seven women.

Harold S. Kushner

Dr. James M. Lawson, Jr.

Harold S. Kushner is rabbi of Temple Israel, Natick, Massachusetts, a position he has held since 1966. He is the author of the bestselling book, *When Bad Things Happen to Good People,* now translated into seven languages. Among his other books are *When All You've Ever Wanted Isn't Enough, When Children Ask About God,* and *Commanded to Live.* Before coming to Natick, the Brooklyn native was an army chaplain and associate rabbi of Temple Israel, Great Neck, New York. He has been a visiting lecturer in Jewish literature at Clark University in Worcester, and is a former editor of *Conservative Judaism* magazine.

Dr. James M. Lawson, Jr., is currently senior pastor at Holman United Methodist Church, the largest United Methodist Church in Los Angeles. He is recognized for his work in movements for justice and dignity, and for his teaching of nonviolence to multitudes of people in many settings. He was one of the founders of the Student Nonviolent Coordinating Committee. In 1958 he became pastor of Centenary United Methodist Church in Memphis, Tennessee, which was visited by Martin Luther King, Jr., at the time of his assasination in 1968. Dr. Lawson's involvement in the civil rights movement is documented in such books as M.L. King's *Why We Can't Wait!* and others.

Madeleine L'Engle

Madeleine L'Engle has taught at the University of Indiana and has been writer-in-residence at Ohio State University, the University of Rochester, and Wheaton College. To date, she has written forty books, including *A Wrinkle in Time* (winner of the Newbery Medal) and *A Swiftly Tilting Planet* (winner of the American Book Award). Some of her other books are *Two-Part Invention, The Glorious Impossible, Sold Into Egypt, Walking on Water: Reflections on Faith and Art,* and *A Stone for a Pillow.* She has received numerous literary awards in the United States, Australia, England, Canada, and Holland.

Dr. Clarice J. Martin

Dr. Clarice J. Martin is Assistant Professor of New Testament at Princeton Theological Seminary. Her research and teaching areas include Luke-Acts, the Synoptic Gospels, and the social origins of earliest Christianity. Among Dr. Martin's recent publications is the annual Presbyterian Women's Bible Study, which is distributed throughout the United States, Korea, and Puerto Rico. A member of numerous organizations and societies, including the American Academy of Religion/Society of Biblical Literature and the Society for the Study of Black Religion, Dr. Martin also serves on the advisory board of the journal *Religion and Intellectual Life*.

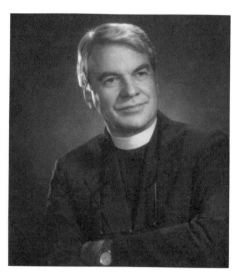

Martin E. Marty

Martin E. Marty is a Lutheran clergyman who, after serving a parish in the Chicago area, became Professor of the History of Modern Christianity at the University of Chicago Divinity School. He is also president of the Park Ridge Center, an organization dedicated to the interface of medicine and religion; editor and senior editor of *The Christian Century* magazine; and coeditor of the journal *Christian History*. Recognized as the premier interpreter of religion in American life, Dr. Marty has written more than thirty books, including *The Righteous Empire* (winner of the National Book Award), *The New Shape of American Religion*, and *Protestantism in the United States* (the first of a multi-volume project on "Modern American Religion").

Daniel P. Matthews

Daniel P. Matthews is rector of the historic Parish of Trinity Church located at the head of Wall Street in New York City. He is also chairman of the board of VISN, an interfaith cable television station. Previously he served as rector of St. Luke's Episcopal Church in Atlanta, one of the largest Episcopal churches in the United States. He has also held positions in Knoxville, Nashville, Memphis, and Monteagle, Tennessee.

Virginia Ramey Mollenkott

Robert Raines

Virginia Ramey Mollenkott was raised in a Protestant fundamentalist family and has had a lifelong attraction to theology, although she earned her degree in seventeenth-century English literature. It was not until she became a feminist that she developed a second specialization in Christian feminist theology. True to her evangelical heritage, she has documented her "radicalization by the Bible" in many articles and in a series of books, among them *Women, Men, and the Bible, Is the Homosexual My Neighbor? Another Christian View* (with Letha Scanzoni), *The Divine Feminine: Biblical Imagery of God as Female, and Godding: Human Responsibility and the Bible*. She served as a stylistic consultant for the New International Version of the Bible, and was a member of the National Council of Churches' committee that prepared *An Inclusive Language Lectionary*. She is currently Professor of English at the William Paterson College of New Jersey.

Robert Raines, a United Methodist pastor and writer, is director of Kirkridge, a retreat center in the mountains of eastern Pennsylvania. From this quiet post in the hills, Dr. Raines has authored popular books of Christian meditation. His bestselling classic, *A Faithing Oak,* has become a source-text for many preachers. Today, Kirkridge remains a thriving retreat center that attracts members of congregations and parishes from around the country.

Rosemary Radford Ruether

Rosemary Radford Ruether is a Roman Catholic theologian who teaches at Garrett Evangelical Theological Seminary in Evanston, Illinois. She has also taught at Harvard, Yale, and Howard Universities. She is recognized world-wide for pioneering a feminist per-spective on theology. Through her writings, she has challenged an entire generation of theologians to break through the patriarchal mindset of the Bible to discover new Christian sym-bols of universal meaning. Dr. Ruether serves on the editorial board of sever-al national journals, among them *Christianity and Crisis* and *The Ecumenist.* Her books include *Sexism and God-Talk: Toward a Feminist Theology* and *New Woman/New Earth*. She has contributed to and edited three major anthologies on women and religious history: *Religion and Sexism, Women and Spirit,* and *Women and Religion in America.*

Valerie Russell

Valerie Russell is president of the City Mission Society of Boston—the first woman and the first layperson to head CMS, which was founded in 1816 and is the second oldest voluntary social service agency in the United States. An urban affairs specialist with particular interest in the application of religion to social issues, Dr. Russell has lectured in theology at Union Theological Seminary (New York) and Yale Divinity School, and since 1982 has taught urban ministry at Harvard Divinity School.

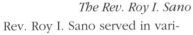
The Rev. Roy I. Sano

The Rev. Roy I. Sano served in various pastoral roles for nineteen years (1950-1969) in California and New York City, followed by fifteen years of work in academic settings. He was a member of the faculty and chaplain at Mills College, Oakland. In 1972, he helped organize the Pacific and Asian American Center for Theology and Strategies (PACTS). From 1975 to 1984, he served as Professor of Theology and Pacific and Asian American Ministries at Pacific School of Religion, Berkeley. He was elected to his present position as bishop of the Denver Area of the United Methodist Church in 1984. His books include *From Every Nation Without Number* and *Outside the Gate: A Study of the Epistle to the Hebrews.*

Susan Schnur

Susan Schnur is an ordained Reconstructionist rabbi (Reconstructionist Judaism is an observance similar to Conservative and Reformed observance, but more inclusive than either and willing to work with less conventional images and beliefs). She is a frequent contributor to the *New York Times, Time,* and other periodicals. She was formerly rabbi at the Jewish Center at Belle Mead, New Jersey, chaplain at the Lawrenceville School, and Professor of Religion and Philosophy at Colgate University. Currently she is editor of *Lilith*, a Jewish feminist magazine, and is completing work on a doctorate in clinical psychology.

Bernard S. Siegel, M.D.

In 1978, Bernard S. Siegel, M.D., started ECap (Exceptional Cancer Patients), a center devoted to a specialized form of individual and group therapy to facilitate personal change and healing. This experience led to his desire to make everyone aware of his or her own healing potential. His bestselling book *Love, Medicine, and Miracles* deals with lessons learned about self-healing, as does his more recent book *Peace, Love, and Healing.* Dr. Siegel has written over twenty-five articles that have appeared in such periodicals as *Psychology Today, Redbook,* and *Family Health.*

The Rt. Rev. John Shelby Spong

The Rt. Rev. John Shelby Spong is Episcopal Bishop of the Diocese of Newark, New Jersey. He is best known in the Anglican community for his fearless leadership in working for the recognition and empowerment of the homosexual community within the church. His views on sexuality and evangelism have challenged the church to look beyond tradition and doctrine, as expressed in his bestselling book *Living in Sin?*

The Rt. Rev. Desmond Tutu

John W. Vannorsdall

The Rt. Rev. Desmond Tutu, Archbishop of Capetown, is also the General Secretary of the South African Council of Churches. Well known around the world for his leadership in the struggle for nonviolent liberation in South Africa, he was awarded the Nobel Peace Prize in 1984. In addition, Bishop Tutu has received honorary doctorates from Harvard and Columbia Universities, and was the recipient of the New York Council of Churches 1983 Family of Man award. He has authored several books, including *Crying in the Wilderness* and *Hope and Suffering,* and was a contributor to *Apartheid Is a Heresy.*

After graduation from seminary, John W. Vannorsdall served two rural churches in western New York State and was later called to Trinity Lutheran Church in New Haven, Connecticut. The remainder of his ministry was spent in academic institutions, first as the Lutheran campus pastor at Cornell, then as chaplain at Gettysburg College during the sixties and seventies. In 1976 he was named university chaplain at Yale. In 1986, he became president of the Lutheran Seminary at Philadelphia, a position he held until retirement in 1990. Dr. Vannorsdall is best known as one of the two Lutheran preachers on the radio broadcast "The Protestant Hour," and through his book *Dimly Burning Wicks.*

Dan Wakefield

Jim Wallis

Dan Wakefield is the author of such popular novels of the 1970s as *Going All the Way* and *Starting Over* (the movie was adapted from his book). He has also written several other books, including *Island in the City: The World of Spanish Harlem* and *Selling Out*. His recent work, *Returning: A Spiritual Journey,* is an autobiographical odyssey of his journey from alcohol addition to the restoration of his faith as a practicing Unitarian. His recent essays in the *New York Times* have covered such topics as men and prayer, Jesus at Harvard, and the emergence of God as a character in contemporary literature.

Jim Wallis is the founder of the Sojourners Community in Washington, D.C. A longtime advocate of the poor and oppressed, Wallis and his fellow community members take a "hands-on" approach to the oppressed by living among them. Mr. Wallis is editor and publisher of *Sojourners* magazine, an internationally recognized publication supporting Christian social action. He is the author of *Agenda for Biblical People: A New Focus for Developing a Lifestyle of Discipleship, Called to Conversion: Recovering the Gospel for These Times,* and *Peacemakers: Christian Voices from the New Abolitionist Movement.*

Dr. Peggy Way

Dr. Peggy Way has served on the faculties of Vanderbilt University Divinity School, The University of Chicago Divinity School, the Jesuit School of Theology, and McCormick Theological Seminary, in addition to her current post at Eden Theological Seminary in Webster Groves, Missouri. A United Church of Christ clergyperson, she has been a member of the Faith and Order Commission of the World Council of Churches, the executive committee of the Consultation on Church Union, and a voting member of the Disciples' Council on Christian Unity.

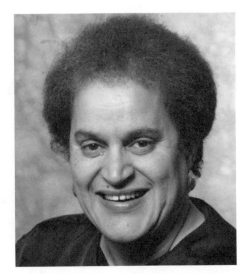

Delores S. Williams

Delores S. Williams is Assistant Professor of Theology and Culture at the Theological School at Drew University in Madison, New Jersey. She has previously taught at Union Theological Seminary (New York), Boston University School of Theology, Fisk University, and Muhlenberg College. Her major interests are reflected in her book *Hagar's Children: New Directions for Black Theology* and *Feminist Theology*. Her articles have appeared in the *Journal of Feminist Thought in Religion, Christianity and Crisis, The Christian Century, Sojourners,* and other periodicals.

Walter Wink

Walter Wink is Professor of Theology at Auburn Seminary in New York. He is known for developing a Socratic approach to teaching the Bible, which enables people to discover truth and meaning for themselves. His book, *Transforming Bible Study,* has become a classic for clergy and lay teachers of the Bible. Dr. Wink conducts workshops worldwide, exploring biblical interpretation as well as issues of justice. His other books include *The Bible in Human Transformation: Towards a New Paradigm for Biblical Study, Naming the Powers: The Language of Power in the New Testament,* and *Unmasking the Powers: The Invisible Forces That Determine Human Existence.*